Presented to

_____

By

_____

On the Occasion of

_____

Date

_____

WHEN
GOD
SEES ME
THROUGH

Devotional Thoughts
on God's Faithfulness
for Women

ANITA CORRINE
DONIHUE

BARBOUR
PUBLISHING, INC.
Uhrichsville, Ohio

Published by Barbour Publishing, Inc., P.O. Box 719, Uhrichsville, Ohio 44683 http://www.barbourbooks.com

ecpa Member of the
Evangelical Christian
Publishers Association

Printed in the United States of America.

WHEN

GOD

SEES ME

THROUGH

DEDICATION

Special thanks to my wonderful sons,
beloved daughters-in-law,
and cherished grandchildren
for their inspiration and encouragement,
and for always believing in me.

Contents

INTRODUCTION

*The LORD is my shepherd; I shall not want. He
maketh me to lie down in green pastures: he
leadeth me beside the still waters. He restoreth
my soul: he leadeth me in the paths of righteousness for his name's sake. Yea, though I walk
through the valley of the shadow of death, I will
fear no evil: for thou art with me; thy rod and
thy staff they comfort me. Thou preparest a table
before me in the presence of mine enemies: thou
anointest my head with oil; my cup runneth
over. Surely goodness and mercy shall follow me
all the days of my life: and I will dwell in the
house of the LORD for ever.* PSALM 23 KJV

Truly, You are my Shepherd, Lord Jesus. Thank You
for how You care for me and supply my needs. You
speak, and I hear Your voice. I listen as You teach me
how to be a Christian shepherd to others.

You make me stop along my hurried way to lie
down in green pastures. I drink of Your pure, sweet,
living water from quiet streams and feel Your peace.

I pour out my concerns to You and give You my
hurts. I feel Your healing presence as You tenderly
restore my soul.

I praise You for leading me to make wise and
righteous decisions. Thank You for reminding me to
put Your will before mine. Your way is always sure
and true.

I long to do Your will, Lord. When the tasks I face are far beyond my wisdom and abilities, I draw on Your guidance and strength.

When I face loss, grief, and even death, I am comforted. You have already walked that valley before me and paid the price to bring me through. No matter how frightening the situation, I need not fear. You are with me.

Thank You for Your comfort and direction, Lord, for guiding me through the challenges and changes in my life.

As I learn to obey, You give me blessings beyond measure, even in the presence of those who are thoughtless and cruel. I praise You as You anoint and continually fill me with Your powerful Holy Spirit, until my cup overflows.

I know Your goodness and mercy will be with me my whole life. Because of Your love, I will always be a part of the family of God.

I will serve You all of my days, and I look forward with great joy to the day You take me home to be with You forever.

The Lord
Is My
Shepherd

HE CARES

"As the Father loved Me, I also have loved you; abide in My love. If you keep My commandments, you will abide in My love, just as I have kept My Father's commandments and abide in His love." JOHN 15:9–10 NKJV

"I am the good shepherd; and I know My sheep, and am known by My own. As the Father knows Me, even so I know the Father; and I lay down My life for the sheep." JOHN 10:14–15 NKJV

"Come, follow me." MARK 1:17 NIV

JESUS CARES FOR US

There is no doubt how much Jesus cares for each of us. He assures us He is our good Shepherd. He is the entrance or the gate to our salvation. He calls us to follow Him so we won't be scattered like lost sheep. When we yield, He draws us safely into His fold. We can go in and out and find secure pasture. He changes our lives from sin and chaos to abundant joy and peace.

Some say shepherds gathered their sheep into the fold for the night, then lay by the gate through the night to protect them. Being a shepherd like David during Bible times must have taken great strength. The shepherds would have had to go through steep mountains and hot, dry valleys; they would have fought off wild animals.

A few years ago, I had the privilege of flying by helicopter over alplike country in Montana. I saw herds of sheep grazing throughout the area with dedicated dogs standing guard on high vantage points or gathering sheep together.

Jesus tells of a good shepherd who had one hundred sheep in his care. The shepherd discovered one lost. He left the other ninety-nine in a safe place and went in search of the one missing. Over craggy mountains he climbed. Down the steep banks into hot, dry valleys he went. Searching. Calling. The shepherd found his sheep and carried it home on his shoulders, rejoicing with each step.

Think of how much more Jesus loves and cares for you and me. When we lose our way, He won't give up until He brings us safely to His fold.

We are the ones who strayed away like sheep!
We, who left God's paths to follow our own.
Yet God laid on him the guilt and sins of every
one of us!

ISAIAH 53:6 TLB

The Ninety and Nine

There were ninety and nine that safely lay
In the shelter of the fold.
But one was out on the hills away,
Far off from the gates of gold.
Away on the mountains wild and bare.
Away from the tender Shepherd's care.
Away from the tender Shepherd's care.

"Lord, Thou hast here Thy ninety and nine;
Are they not enough for Thee?"
But the Shepherd made answer: "This of Mine
Has wandered away from Me;
And although the road be rough and steep,
I go to the desert to find My sheep,
I go to the desert to find My sheep."

And all through the mountains, thunder riven
And up from the rocky steep,
There arose a glad cry to the gate of heaven,
"Rejoice! I have found My sheep!"
And the angels echoed around the throne,
"Rejoice, for the Lord brings back His own!
"Rejoice, for the Lord brings back His own!"

Elizabeth Cecelia Douglas Clephane, 1868

THANK YOU FOR YOUR CARE

Thank You, Father, for loving us like the lost sheep and never giving up on us. I praise You for Your goodness and mercy that endure forever.

You loved us so much that You willingly gave Your only Son to die for us. We give You our hearts and lives, and You save us from sin and destruction.

Thank You for loving us as much as You do Your own Son. I will gladly abide in Your love and stay near Your sheltering fold.

HIS VOICE

"The watchman opens the gate for him, and the sheep listen to his voice. He calls his own sheep by name and leads them out. When he has brought out all his own, he goes on ahead of them, and his sheep follow him because they know his voice." JOHN 10:3–4 NIV

HEARING HIS VOICE

The weather didn't look threatening when I took my elementary students out for recess. My class joined the others in enthusiastic play, shouting and laughing as loudly as they could. I was pleased they were able to run off some energy.

Halfway through recess, black, threatening clouds like a dark gray curtain worked their way in our direction. In seconds, the sky opened up with pelting rain, pushed by hard winds. The children aimlessly dashed in every direction. From under the school's eaves, I shouted their names to follow me. I was amazed how my voice cut through the chaotic noise of wind, rain, and screeching children to reach each child's ear. It wasn't long until all followed me inside to warmth and safety.

I used to wonder how our high school basketball players could hear directions at our games. High-pitched emotions cause spectators to stand in the bleachers and scream themselves hoarse. Drums bang. Horns blow. But the trusted coach calls out instructions, and the team members recognize his voice and follow his directions.

In our daily walk with God we pray and read His Word. We listen as He strengthens, comforts, and guides. The more we stay close to God, the more we recognize His voice. When storms of life and confusion blow and people aimlessly run here and there, we know to fine-tune our spiritual ears to His instructions. His peace and order surround us, when we listen and obey. Before we know it, He has brought us under His wings into warmth and safety.

Jesus Calls Us

Jesus calls us o'er the tumult
Of our life's wild, restless, sea;
Day by day His sweet voice soundeth,
Saying, "Christian, follow Me."

In our joys and in our sorrows,
Days of toil and hours of ease,
Still He calls, in cares and pleasures,
"Christian, love Me more than these!"

CECIL FRANCES HUMPHREYS ALEXANDER, 1852

Let Me Hear Your Voice

Lord, this is one of those chaotic days. As I go about my duties, please let me hear Your still, small voice. I know You well, because I love You and want to follow Your lead.

Cut through the hurry and fuss—guide me, I pray. Help me to be calm. Remind me to react politely (especially to my dear family) during these frustrating moments. Allow me to not go ahead of You. Lead me.

Thank You, Lord, for staying near me and guiding me with Your still, calming voice.

I Shall
Not Want

HOPELESSNESS

*Behold, the eye of the LORD is on those who
fear Him, On those who hope for His lovingkindness. . . . Let Thy lovingkindness, O
LORD, be upon us, According as we have hoped
in Thee.*

PSALM 33:18, 22 NAS

HOPELESSNESS
AWAKENS THE HEART

Dwight L. Moody told about an experience of an
Englishman who lived in Chicago in the winter
before the great fire. The man observed rapid growth
in the forty-year-old city. Impressed by its magnifi-
cent buildings, churches, and schools, he decided to
report his findings to folks in Manchester and surrounding areas. However, no one shared his interest
in Chicago.

One day the news spread about Chicago's cata-
strophic fire. All seemed hopeless. Half of the city
was burned. Reports came over the news that over
100,000 people were homeless and nearly starving.
They desperately needed help.

People were shocked when they heard the news.
Everyone began showing concern for the afflicted in
Chicago. Thousands responded. Citizens from other

towns assisted with money, muscle, and compassion. Now, others became interested in the city of Chicago.

So it is in our lives. When things are hopeless and we don't know which way to turn, God uses what has happened to bring out the best in us. He works it together for good. He replaces despair with hope and confidence for the future.

WE HAVE A HOPE

Blessed hope we have within us is an anchor
    to our soul,
It is both steadfast and sure.
It is founded on the promises of Father's
    written word,
And 'twill evermore endure.
We have a hope within our souls,
Brighter than the perfect day;
God has given us His Spirit,
And we want the world to hear it,
All our doubts are passed away.

WILLIAM G. SCHELL, 1926

You Are My Hope

My hope is nearly gone, Lord. I have reached my lowest ebb. I feel totally cast down. Do You care about me in this busy world? Do others know I need help?

Although everything seems hopeless, Lord, Your Bible assures me nothing is impossible when I put my trust in You. I won't allow myself to dwell on the negative. I will completely leave this problem in Your hands.

Thank You for changing my perspective from despair to hope and confidence in You.

When We Have Needs

God will supply every need of yours according to his riches in glory in Christ Jesus.
PHILIPPIANS 4:19 RSV

The Right Car

Dana hustled out the front door to leave for school where she taught an elementary class. She quickly unlocked the door of her old Toyota and threw in her bag and purse. In rapid succession, Dana ran to the front of the car, expertly unhooked the electric battery charger, opened the garage door, and put the charger away. With a quick flip of the hand, she pulled down the garage door and popped her hood shut. Dana was on her way.

In spite of the battery problems, she loved her little car and was thankful for it. It practically manufactured gas. She and her husband, Wes, were planning to buy an alternator out of their next paychecks.

But even though she appreciated her car, when Dana wheeled into a parking spot at school, she felt embarrassed to park near the shiny new beauties in the staff lot. She locked the doors and went into the school.

When Dana returned to her parking spot after school, she stared in disbelief. Her little car had been stolen!

She phoned Wes, and he immediately came to the school to help her. Police and insurance reports were made. The couple carried only the necessary liability insurance on the little clunker. What would they do?

Payday came. Wes and Dana received no news on her missing car. The couple sat at the kitchen table and prayed together about their need. They were determined to still give their tithe to God and trust Him to help them find another car.

After cutting corners and figuring to the penny, Wes and Dana managed to scrape up one thousand dollars. They didn't want to go into debt and hoped it would be enough to buy something safe and reliable.

During the next few days, Wes and Dana drove from one car lot to another in search of something within their price range. No success. They combed the want ads and watched along the streets. Still nothing. Dana asked God to return her little car. All they could do was wait.

Wes still had his car of course, so he drove Dana to school and picked her up. This made both of their schedules difficult. When would God answer their prayers?

One evening Dana told her friend Sherry about the stolen car. Sherry's face lit up.

Two years before, Sherry's grandmother sadly came to the point of not being able to drive anymore. Her grandmother hadn't been able to bring herself to sell the car until now. Dana remembered meeting the nice elderly lady at the hospital, when Sherry had one of her babies. Sherry's grandmother and Dana had chatted briefly. Now, Sherry explained, her grandmother wanted to sell her car for twenty-five hundred dollars.

Dana knew that was too much for her and Wes, but she thanked Sherry for the thought.

"Let me talk with her," Sherry offered.

Dana felt Sherry's grandmother deserved the full price for her car; buying it would be out of the question. To Dana's surprise, Sherry's grandmother agreed to one thousand dollars! She wanted her car to go to someone special and have a good owner.

Dana was thrilled beyond words when Wes and Sherry's husband pulled into the driveway with a fairly new, fully automatic silver Toyota. It had power everything, a great radio, and a tape player. Dana thanked Sherry, her grandmother, and God for the wonderful gift. The Lord had supplied Dana's needs and more than met her wants.

The police located her stolen car right after Wes and Dana bought the new one. It had been wrecked and was now worthless. Wes and Dana are glad they were faithful in tithing to God and remained out of debt. Most of all, they are thankful for His supplying their need.

UNSEARCHABLE RICHES

Oh, the unsearchable riches of Christ,
Wealth that can never be told!
Riches exhaustless of mercy and grace,
Precious, more precious than gold!

FRANCES JANE (FANNY) CROSBY, 1820–1915

THANK YOU FOR
MEETING MY NEEDS

Here I am again, Lord, presenting my needs to You. I think back on many times You remembered me with Your favor. Now I put my hope in You as I wait on Your answer.

I bring You my cares now and will obey Your will. Thank You for Your blessings to come, beyond measure, pressed down, shaken together, and overflowing.

He Makes Me to Lie Down in Green Pastures

STRESS

Humble yourselves, therefore, under God's mighty hand, that he may lift you up in due time. Cast all your anxiety on him because he cares for you.   1 PETER 5:6–7 NIV

ALL THINGS TO ALL PEOPLE

Frank's death grip finally released, and he let the phone receiver fall into the cradle. How could he help his friend Marty solve his problems? No matter how Frank tried to help, Marty's life kept going in circles.

Frank returned to his computer, hoping to complete an extra project. It was already three hours past quitting time, and he wanted to go home and be with his family.

The phone rang. Frank cringed. "What now," he muttered. Frank took care of someone else's problem and hung up. Anxiety flashed over him. "Lord, I want to help people and go the second mile. I know You tell me to be used of God, but these problems are stressing me out to the max. What can I do?"

Frank let the screen saver cover his work as he leaned back in his office chair. He thought about how he constantly tried to find solutions for other people's dilemmas. Could he be hindering God's will in their lives? Was he acting as a crutch to them? He loved his friends, but was he really helping them?

Frank reflected on the nights of sleep he had lost pacing the floor with concern. He realized he was robbing himself of the strength and energy he wanted to give to Linda and his children.

Frank closed his eyes and saw the sweetest wife and children ever—his own. Certainly, they were more important to him, and they must come first.

He reached in his desk drawer and pulled out his Bible. Reading one Scripture after another, he knew what he must do.

Laying down his Bible, Frank called on the Lord again. He took the needs of his friends to God in prayer. He willingly let go and left the problem solving to God.

After he finished praying, Frank pulled out a sheet of paper. He wrote the names of all those who relied heavily on him and listed ways he could step back and trust God and his friends to solve their problems. Frank asked for guidance again. He formed a plan on how to delegate extra work projects being thrown his way.

When he finished, Frank shut the computer down. He picked up the phone and dialed home.

"Honey, are you still up? I'm stopping for our favorite ice cream on my way home. I'm leaving now. How about a dish with someone who loves you? I have something great to tell you."

Frank hung up. Funny. This time he didn't have a death grip on the phone. Instead, he felt relieved and filled with peace.

"Take My yoke upon you, and learn from Me, for I am gentle and humble in heart; and you shall find rest for your souls. For My yoke is easy, and My load is light."

MATTHEW 11:29–30 NAS

LEANING ON
THE EVERLASTING ARMS

What have I to dread, what have I to fear,
Leaning on the everlasting arms;
I have blessed peace with my Lord so near,
Leaning on the everlasting arms.

ELISHA ALBRIGHT HOFFMAN, 1887

ROLLING OVER THE STRESS

Father, thank You for encouraging me to let go of things. I will, instead, trust You to handle these problems.

Each time I'm tempted to take on more than I should, I pray that You will help me gain new perspective about what is really important in my life. When the pressures come and I have done all I should do, let me roll over my worries and place them in Your faithful hands. Thank You for replacing the stress in my life with security in You.

FATIGUE

But those who wait on the Lord Shall renew their strength; They shall mount up with wings like eagles, They shall run and not be weary, They shall walk and not faint.

ISAIAH 40:31 NKJV

FATIGUE-BUSTER HOUSE

Bobbie's first semester of college sped by. She worked long, hard hours to maintain her 4.0 GPA. She wanted to meet the standards to qualify for law school.

But her studies became more difficult during the second semester. Words on the pages blurred. Her energy level dropped at an alarming rate. She felt bone-tired and ached all over.

Bobbie excused herself from doing things with

her friends. Meals in the cafeteria were replaced with a snack and Coke next to her books. It had been months since she had gone home to see her family— or even gone to church.

When Bobbie's mom or dad called, she talked like everything was fine and assured them of her excellent grades. She brushed off their questions about her health and activities.

One afternoon Bobbie's twin brother, Brad, called. She knew she couldn't fool him. He knew her too well. Through their younger years, they shared everything.

After a few leading questions from Brad, Bobbie opened up. Between sobs, she told him how hard she was trying and about her extreme fatigue. Brad's familiar "all-will-be-well" voice zoomed through the phone lines and comforted her. "It's going to be all right, Sis. Hey, tune in to the Christian radio station tonight at ten o'clock. I hear there's going to be someone talking about a surefire fatigue buster for people like us overachievers. I love you, Sis, and I will be praying for you. I'll call in a couple of nights."

When ten o'clock rolled around, Bobbie flipped on her radio and listened while continuing to study. She wondered what could help more than caffeine.

"Are you reaching for the stars to accomplish your dreams and goals? Are you missing the mark because of fatigue? Allow me to help you turn it all around. Let me tell you about God's fatigue buster."

Bobbie listened halfheartedly and continued to

study. "What does he know?" she mumbled.

When the speaker described Bobbie's lifestyle to the last detail, however, she put down her book and listened.

"Think of your life like a nice, strong house," the radio voice continued. "Matthew 7:24–27 says a good home is built on a solid foundation. We must check our lives and be sure they're based on God's strong principles."

Bobbie nodded. *That makes sense.*

"Read Hebrews 12:1–3. Take time for walks or runs. Exercise reduces stress and fatigue, and it gets the blood circulating far better than caffeine."

Bobbie laughed and wondered if this radio announcer had read her mind.

"Open the front door. Let the sunlight and fresh air in, rather than always being boxed inside. Look up Psalm 89:15. Try changing your work environment to a deck or near a window. Open your heart and let the light of God flow in.

"Step into the kitchen. Daniel chapter 1 encourages us to find the foods we need that give strength and good health.

"Read Proverbs 3:1–6. Draw up a reasonable schedule for your week. Allow time for daily devotions and prayer. Fill your mind with good, uplifting things.

"Read Nehemiah 8:10. Have some fun with your friends. They add zest and joy to your life.

"Read Proverbs 3:21–24. Get adequate sleep. It

helps you think clearly and make sound decisions.

"In Exodus 23:12 the Bible tells us to work six days and rest on the seventh. Go to church so you can keep your heart and mind focused on the right things. Spend the rest of that day enjoying your family and friends. Remember, *don't* work. When the next day comes, throw yourself full speed ahead into your labor.

"Look at Colossians 3:23–24. Make your time count so you can enjoy your work and the other special things in your life.

"This," the speaker concluded, "will be your best fatigue buster ever."

Bobbie didn't wait for Brad to call. She turned off her radio and phoned him immediately. "Thanks, Brad." She sighed. "Now I have the answer to my problem. I'm going to start making changes in my life right away."

After she hung up, Bobbie called her parents and asked if they would be home the following weekend. She wanted to come visit.

Bobbie's energy level increased over the next few days. Not only was her fatigue disappearing, she could think clearly again. She finished her schoolwork in half the time.

Bobbie graduated from law school, passed the bar exam, and is now a successful Christian lawyer. She still practices what she learned from her "fatigue-buster house" and passes the lessons on to other hardworking people.

And so, dear brothers, I plead with you to give your bodies to God. Let them be a living sacrifice, holy—the kind he can accept. When you think of what he has done for you, is this too much to ask? Don't copy the behavior and customs of this world, but be a new and different person with a fresh newness in all you do and think. Then you will learn from your own experience how his ways will really satisfy you.

ROMANS 12:1–2 TLB

TAKE MY LIFE AND LET IT BE

Take my life, and let it be consecrated,
    Lord, to Thee.
Take my moments and my days;
Let them flow in ceaseless praise.

FRANCES RIDLEY HAVERGAL, 1873

CHANGE MY FATIGUE
TO FULFILLMENT

Lord, I earnestly seek You in my time of need. I'm tired. My body aches. My soul longs for Your strength and direction. Grant me energy, I pray.

Show me a new lifestyle. Remind me to use Your precepts in all my ways so I don't fret and give up.

Thank You for teaching me how to change my fatigue to energy and fulfillment.

PLEASANT PLACES

Be at rest once more, O my soul, for the LORD has been good to you.   PSALM 116:7 NIV

ESCAPING TO GOD

In our busiest and most stressful weeks, some of us take a few moments to daydream about a quiet bubble bath with a good book.

If you had the chance to escape, where would you like to go? The moon or quiet outer space? An airplane ride to watch the sun sink behind the pink, cotton-candy clouds? How about a cruise? Hawaii?

Deep-sea diving with the dolphins? Relaxing on the beach under the warm sun while waves lap your toes? Floating down a lazy river, or riding the exciting rapids? Watching wildlife in a remote field?

I would love to do all these, but one of my favorite time-outs is catching a sunset or sunrise in my own backyard with my husband, my best friend. Years ago, our youngest son, Dave, and I used to camp in the backyard. Staying in the tent wasn't our cup of tea. We loved it under the stars.

We would lie there for hours talking and straining to stay awake, knowing we could see shooting stars from midnight until early morning. Whispering with excitement, we counted them. The next day we felt refreshed and invigorated by our late-night getaway.

The greatest escapes of all are when we spend time with our dearest Friend, the Lord Jesus. He's a wonderful listener. After we talk with Him and wait a little while, He speaks to our hearts and shows us amazing things. We leave feeling refreshed.

Vacations are wonderful, but they are complete when we escape to time alone with God. No matter where we go, He is there.

The next time you are "getting away," take your Bible so you can find a quiet, pleasant place and enjoy it with the Lord. What a wonderful escape it will be!

LORD,
THOU HAST SEARCHED ME

Lord, Thou has searched me and dost know
Where'er I rest, where'er I go;
Thou knowest all that I have planned,
And all my ways are in Thy hand.
If I the wings of morning take,
And far away my dwelling make,
The hand that leadeth me is Thine,
And my support Thy power divine.

THE PSALTER, 1912

ESCAPING TO YOU

I love escaping to You, Lord. No matter where I go,
You are there. Thank You for listening and then
touching my heart.

In Your presence, I find a pleasant resting place.
I read Your Word and listen. You speak to my heart,
and I feel peace.

Thank You for this pleasant place You prepared
for me, Lord. I feel refreshed and refilled. Stay with
me as I leave. I look forward to the next time I can
return and meet with You.

He Leads Me beside the Still Waters

SEEKING GOD'S WILL

*Jesus said to him, "I am the way, the truth,
and the life. No one comes to the Father except
through Me."*   JOHN 14:6 NKJV

GUIDE TO SAFETY

Tom and Renee planned for months to take a one-
day hike into the Cascade Mountains.

On the day before their hike, the couple orga-
nized their supplies. Tom loaded his large backpack
with a cell phone, food, flashlight, compass, binoculars, map, and a knife for safety. Renee filled her
smaller backpack with a camera, a small Bible, clean
socks, warm clothing, two insulated blankets, and
water bottles.

Early the next morning Tom and Renee drove
out to the starting point of their hike. They normally
recorded their names at a state park registry. Since it
was a beautiful August day and they expected to
return in a few hours, they decided to not worry
about it.

The sun peeked over the eastern horizon, creat-
ing diamonds on the nearby river. Soft, cool breezes
invited the couple up the ascending trail. Wildflowers laced with dew lined the path with colorful
blossoms, slowly unfolding their tiny petals.

Tom and Renee took a moderate, steady pace, humming "This Is My Father's World" in time to their steps. The sun climbed higher. It wrapped its warm blanket around the hikers. Small animals scampered about, scolding the couple for invading their territory.

After a few hours, Tom and Renee decided to stop for a snack. Renee pulled out the camera and took some shots of the river ribboning through the valley. Tom noticed an intriguing side trail. He checked the map and discovered the smaller trail would take them into the woods and near interesting caves.

Renee squinted at the map over Tom's arm. "Are you sure it's safe?"

Adventurous sparks flashed in Tom's eyes. "It looks harmless enough. Let's hike in a couple hours and break for lunch."

Emerald trees hugged the smaller trail as Tom and Renee trudged farther up the hillside. The early afternoon sun crept high above them. A warm breeze caressed their faces. Birds chirped while hustling about their business. Hawks and an occasional eagle glided overhead.

The hikers found a clearing and stopped for lunch. Tom slung off his backpack and pulled out their food. Renee stood nearby, breathing in the fresh, sweet air. Soon she would get out their water bottles and Bible. What a perfect spot to worship God.

Before Renee had a chance to remove her pack, the nearby bushes rustled. Was it a small animal? A heartbeat later, their eyes popped wide open. It wasn't a small animal, but a large bear. And it was coming straight toward them.

"He smells food!" Tom shouted.

"Let him have it," Renee shrilled.

They joined hands and backed away. The bear shuffled back and forth as though trying to decide which way to go—after the food or after the people!

Tom and Renee took no chances. They ran to the nearest climbable trees, surprised at how fast two adults could scramble. They perched on the branches and hung on tightly. The obviously upset bear circled and pushed on the tree trunks. At last it made its way to Tom's pack.

Renee's anger flared. "How dare you, Bear? That's our lunch!" She balanced herself against her tree trunk and pulled out her camera. Aiming for the bear, she hurled the camera as hard as she could. It spiraled through the air and landed soundly on the bear's nose.

The bear let out a yelp and a grunt, then disappeared with Tom's pack into the bushes, pieces of lunch trailing behind.

An eternity later, the terrified couple inched their way down to the welcome ground. Renee gathered up her dusty camera. Tom cleaned up the mess left by the bear.

Now they didn't even have a phone to call for help. Darkness settled in. It was too dangerous to attempt the hike back until first signs of light, *before* a certain bear awakened, so Tom and Renee wrapped themselves in warm clothing and blankets. They huddled beneath a tree, quoting Bible verses and praying.

Hours later, slivers of light shimmered in the clear sky. Tom checked the fading stars. It didn't take long to regain his directional bearings. The weary hikers gingerly worked their way down the trail and thanked God when they finally spotted the river and their car.

Spiritual Survival Kit

Do you ever grasp for answers when you reach a fork in life's road? Do you wonder what God wants you to do, or if He's calling you at all? It's often best at this time to retreat into God's presence and wait for His direction. When we turn to Him, He has a way of making things fall into place and helping us find our way.

God provides us with a spiritual survival kit filled with directions for our lives. Better than Tom's knife, the Bible is a double-edged sword (Eph. 6:17) helping us cut to the truth God has for us. Jesus tells us in John 6:35 that He is the Bread of Life. Psalm 119:105 shows how God's Word lights our path. Like Tom's compass, the Scripture gives us direction (Ps. 32:7–8) and places a perimeter around us— guarding us and setting limits.

Instead of giving us binoculars (Acts 2:17), the Lord helps us visualize His directions. His map guides us on straight paths (Prov. 3:6). In Psalm 51:10, we're encouraged to pray for a clean heart, symbolic of the clean water Renee carried.

When we feel afraid, Psalm 91:4 assures that God will wrap His loving arms around us, like the hikers' insulated blankets, comforting and protecting us. Psalm 36:8 tells how He guides us to His rivers of delight. We become refreshed, strengthened, and focused on Him. He shows us the way to serve Him, just as He showed Tom and Renee the way home.

THE LORD IS MY SHEPHERD

My soul crieth out, "Restore me again.
And give me the strength to take
The narrow path of righteousness,
E'en for His own name's sake."

RALPH E. HUDSON, 1885

I WILL FOLLOW YOU

Show me the ways You want me to go, O Lord. Keep my paths right and true. Guide me with Your truth and righteousness.

When I mess up, thank You for being here and helping me back to the right path. I will follow You all my life and bless Your name forever.

PEACE

Grace to you and peace from God the Father and our Lord Jesus Christ.

GALATIANS 1:3 NKJV

SNATCHED AWAY

The last day of school finally arrived. I waved good-bye to my students and tackled my work to finish the school year. After several hours of reorganizing, cleaning, packing, and making final preparations for September, I was ready to leave.

I arrived home tired but anxious to dive into my writing and catch up on house and yard work. My mind raced; my body drove on pure willpower.

Bob met me at the door with a big smile and a tall glass of ice water. He recognized the look of exhaustion he had seen so often. "Let's run away," he urged.

"When?" I sighed. "I have a lot of work to do. I want to have this book just right. . . ." My voice trailed off as I felt God coaxing me to stop and tune in.

"Tonight. Now."

"I'm tired," I whined.

Bob didn't seem to hear. Bob is spontaneous and romantic. After forty years of marriage, I've learned to do things on the spur of the moment and have usually been glad we did. I felt God's coaxing again.

"Do you want to?" Bob gazed at me with puppy dog eyes.

I nodded weakly.

Within a half an hour, we had the van loaded with a ready-made bed in back. I packed a small bag of essentials. At the last minute, I tucked in a pen and tablet with a few reminder notes next to my Bible. *Please, God. Help me to find time to write.*

Bob loves adventure. He started driving and asked, "Mountain or water?"

"Either one. Um—water, water sounds good," I mumbled.

"I'll surprise you." We drove for several hours and finally reached our destination in the middle of somewhere. We couldn't find an open campground, so we pulled our van into a well-lit church parking lot. After we positioned the van close to the building, we climbed into our bed in back and slept soundly.

Early the next morning, we awoke to the sun peering through tree leaves and birds chirping a cheerful good morning.

After freshening up in a public restroom and

having breakfast, we found our way to Twanoh State Park near Belfair, Washington. We were still a little tired, so we opted for a short nap. A few moments of rest refreshed me. I slipped quietly out of the van with my tablet and left Bob to rest peacefully. I walked out to the northwest corner of the park and drank in the view of Hood Canal, where the water flows from the Puget Sound. Its clear blue ripples reflected the sunlight as the water wound itself around the point. I found a picnic table distanced from any activity, spread out my work, and began to pray and write.

Few people were out yet, not even a boat turned the water. Some folks quietly searched for oysters in the distance. Wooded foothills of the Olympic Peninsula framed the water. Fluffy, cumulus clouds played across the pale blue sky. The one-mile-wide lake brought to mind the well-known words of Jesus: "Peace, be still."

I felt rested and at peace. My words flew from pen to paper, barely able to keep up with my flowing thoughts. God ministered to my heart as I wrote. After a couple of hours, I heard familiar footsteps crunch in the pebbles behind me. Bob joined me with a welcoming cup of hot chocolate.

He took in a big breath of fresh air and smiled. "How are you doing?" His voice rang with love. "I'm going to a table in the shade to read and listen to some music on my headset."

I felt grateful for the time and peace he so generously allowed me. I continued writing. After a couple more hours, I closed my tablet and joined Bob for the remainder of our peaceful day together.

RIVER OF PEACE

O this river of peace
Makes me perfect and whole;
And its blessings increase,
Flowing deep in my soul.

DANIEL S. WARNER, 1842–1895

THANK YOU FOR
PROVIDING PEACE

Lord, thank You for helping me relax. My energy grows, my thoughts clear. I'm grateful for those who recognize my needs for peace and rest.

Thank You for calling me from a world of hurry, for leading me beside Your still waters, and restoring my body and soul.

He Restores
My Soul

DISCOURAGEMENT

*"Fear not, for I am with you; Be not dismayed,
for I am your God. I will strengthen you, Yes, I
will help you, I will uphold you with My
righteous right hand."*　　ISAIAH 41:10 NKJV

CROSSED PATHS

The three of us united in prayer in the airport parking garage. We asked for protection, guidance, and God's blessing on those with whom we came in contact. Bob was seeing Colleen Reece and me off to Birmingham, Alabama, where we had been asked to speak at Samford University.

When Colleen and I approached the ticket counter, we requested a window seat for one of us. The clerk did a little shuffling and graciously switched our seating assignments. I kissed Bob good-bye, and we boarded the plane. I offered the window seat to Colleen and made myself comfortable in the center seat. We would trade places on our next flight.

Before long, a young man loaded his carry-on bag into the overhead storage compartment and sat down on the other side of me. He appeared extremely nervous. When the jet engines revved in preparation for takeoff, the man's face paled. His knuckles turned white as he gripped the armrests.

I sent up a silent prayer. *What can I do to help?*

The plane climbed, then leveled off. The man remained rigid and tense.

I took a deep breath. "Hi, I'm Anita. Where are you flying to?"

"Texas," he offered. "I'm Matt."

I ventured on. "Do you have family there?"

"My parents. They're celebrating my dad's eightieth birthday. I haven't flown since I was a little kid."

I cracked a few jokes about the heat in Texas and other insignificant things, and Matt appeared a little more relaxed. I introduced Colleen and explained we were Christian authors, on our way to speak in Alabama. Idle chitchat followed. Then silence.

After a couple of minutes, he turned to me. His look had changed from panic to seriousness. "Do you have children?"

I thought of my family and how precious they are to me. "I have several grown children and grandchildren," I replied.

Matt's eyes became watery. His lips trembled. He let go of the armrests and wiped away his overflowing tears. I handed him a couple of napkins and listened while Matt poured out his heart.

Stress was challenging his family's relationship. He and his wife were juggling their careers and struggling to raise two strong-willed teenagers. Although Matt and his wife loved the Lord and went to church, they felt overwhelmed and discouraged. They weren't sure they could remain together.

We talked for the rest of the trip. Colleen rested

quietly and enjoyed the view. I listened, then shared the many lessons God taught me through my studies while writing *When I'm on My Knees*.

"God sees us through the good and bad times," I continued, while Matt listened intently. "When we are the most discouraged, I believe that's when God is closer than ever."

We explored the necessity of trusting God, asking Him to help us through disheartening times, and obeying His will unconditionally. We recalled how the Scriptures tell us we can draw strength and wisdom from God.

"God loves you and your family, Matt. As you trust and obey Him, He will see you through. Things may not go the way you want, but He will take care of you and your family. Remember, nothing is impossible for God."

Matt's face filled with awe. "My seat assignment was changed from a different part of the plane at the last minute. It was no accident that I was placed next to you, was it? I think God planned it this way."

I explained that our seats had also been changed, and I also believed God meant for our paths to cross. We said a quick prayer together for God to help Matt and his family.

As soon as we landed, I pulled a copy of *When I'm on My Knees* from my carry-on bag and handed it to him. "This is for you and your wife. You will be in our thoughts and prayers." Colleen and I gave him hugs and a "God bless you," then we were on our way.

I never saw or heard from Matt again, but I still

marvel at the way God ministered to him during discouraging times and made our paths cross.

God Will Take Care of You

Be not dismayed whatever betide,
God will take care of you;
Beneath His wings of love abide,
God will take care of you.
God will take care of you,
Through every day, over all the way;
He will take care of you,
God will take care of you.
No matter what may be the test,
God will take care of you;
Lean, weary one, upon His breast,
God will take care of you.

CIVILLA DURFEE MARTIN, 1904

Discouragement
Changed to Encouragement

Father, thank You for being with me when I'm
discouraged, for not making me feel guilty for being weak. Where I am weak, You are strong. When
I crumble from stress and trials, You hold me up

with Your righteous hand.

Praise You, Lord, for changing my discouragement to encouragement. Because of Your love and the promises in Your Word, I know You are with me all the time, wherever I go.

ILLNESS

Who Himself bore our sins in His own body on the tree, that we, having died to sins, might live for righteousness—by whose stripes you were healed. 1 PETER 2:24 NKJV

NEVER SAY NEVER

Nine-year-old Samuel waved good-bye and chirped a "See you later" to me at the end of a regular school day. I love the students I help Wendy teach. They warm our hearts as they give their love in return.

Samuel suffered from brain cancer. His illness, surgery, and various treatments took their toll on the sweet little boy. Miraculously, he came through everything with a big smile.

The next morning, Wendy and I received a call from Samuel's mother. Samuel had taken a fall the night before, and afterward he appeared not to recognize anyone in his family. His parents had rushed him to the hospital, but things had grown progressively worse. Samuel was slipping into a coma.

After school, several of the teachers gathered in Wendy's classroom. We formed a circle and took hands. One by one, we bowed our heads, lifting Samuel and his family's needs to God.

The load I felt for Samuel was almost unbearable that night when I entered our church for worship team practice and Bible study. I immediately burst into tears and shared Samuel's needs with our singing group. They clustered around me. Again Samuel was brought to God in fervent prayer.

After music practice, I spilled out Samuel's condition to our home Bible study group. It didn't look good for the little boy's recovery. Why was this happening when he had already come through so much? A hint of doubt entered the group. The words "Maybe it's God's time. . . ." were on the edge of some lips, but they were immediately erased and replaced with "Never say never." We agreed we must trust God and ask for healing.

We lifted our petitions to God more strongly than ever before. We asked for Samuel's healing in the name of Jesus, and we thanked God for the miracles and blessings to come.

Samuel's miracle came. He made a turnaround and regained enough energy to come home from the hospital and return to school.

On his first day back, Samuel entered the classroom with his usual big smile. "I'm ba-a-ck," he said.

He laughed and hugged us. We hugged him and silently thanked God for our answered prayer.

There's another kind of miracle many of us request. Along with prayer for physical healing, we beg for some of our friends and loved ones to accept Jesus as their Savior and Lord. We pray and pray and see no change. Sometimes things become worse. The one we pray for goes deeper into sin. All the signs may point to discouragement, hopelessness, no apparent chance of turning around. In our eyes, the situation looks impossible. We are tempted to give up, write them off, and say they will never change.

At that instant, we must shake off the doubts and never say never. Nothing is impossible when we trust God. It may take a long time, but God works through everything. He never gives up. He loves our friends and loved ones more than we are capable of doing. Unlike us, He can talk to their hearts, and they can't escape His words. There's a spiritual battle going on for the souls of these dear ones. As we present our prayers to God, we can be assured of the One Who wins over sin and destruction.

Some of our prayers may go unanswered while we are still alive. Praise be to God, our prayers lifted to Him go on, even after our lives here on earth are finished! We can look forward to the answers being revealed to us when we reach heaven.

When all is bleak and appears impossible, keep turning your troubles over to God. Never say never. Always say, "Forever, with God!"

HOW FIRM A FOUNDATION

How firm a foundation, ye saints of the Lord,
Is laid for your faith in His excellent Word!
What more can He say than to you He hath said,
You, who unto Jesus for refuge have fled?

JOHN RIPPON'S
*A Selection of Hymns from
the Best Authors,* 1787

YOUR UNFAILING STRENGTH

How marvelous and wonderful are the ways You are
with me, Lord, giving me daily strength. When I am
weak, You are strong. When my faith wavers, You fill
me with Your blessed assurance. No matter how
gigantic the requests I bring, You handle them, Lord.
I stand on Your firm foundation and trust You for
strength and healing.

I depend on Your saving grace as I pray for the
ones dear to me. Thank You for Your promise to
never leave those who trust in You. You are greater
than anything I face. I praise You for being my Lord,
my God.

He Leads Me
in Paths of
Righteousness

RAISING CHILDREN

These commandments that I give you today
are to be upon your hearts. Impress them on
your children. Talk about them when you sit at
home and when you walk along the road,
when you lie down and when you get up. Tie
them as symbols on your hands and bind them
on your foreheads. Write them on the door-
frames of your houses and on your gates.

DEUTERONOMY 6:6–9 NIV

Train a child in the way he should go, and
when he is old he will not turn from it.

PROVERBS 22:6 NIV

MOLDING THE FUTURE

This pastor's wife was a remarkable mother of nine-teen children (only nine lived beyond infancy). She taught each one the basics of education, including Greek and Latin. This dedicated mother made music come alive. Her children learned to read poetry and music, to play musical instruments, and to write and compose music of their own. Love for God, along with education, rated high in her priorities. She was deter-mined to pass on all she knew to her children.

Each child received her discipline and love. When

she punished them, she cried quietly and loved immensely. If they told her the truth, they were never spanked. She spent fifteen minutes alone with each child every day.

Some labeled her stern, forbidding. Yet, she retained love and respect from her huge family. She faithfully prayed for her beloved children. She poured every ounce of wisdom she possessed into their open hearts and minds. She expected the best from them even into adulthood. She charged them to make serving God the center of their lives. She explained it was the most necessary, if not the only, purpose for being.

I wonder if Susanna Wesley knew God was helping her mold the lives of her sons John and Charles and her grandson Samuel S. Wesley into great Christian leaders. The wisdom and love she gave her family multiplied through her offspring's outstanding sermons, poetry, and hymns. Their God-inspired words left a legacy. Timeless words from the Wesley family have endured through generations, and continue to teach and inspire us today.

A CHARGE TO KEEP I HAVE

To serve the present age,
My calling to fulfill:
O may it all my powers engage
To do my Master's will!

CHARLES WESLEY, 1762

Teach Me to Parent

Thank You for my children, Lord. They are my most precious gifts from You. I look at them and see how they reflect different family members—their hair, their eyes, the little dimple like mine. Most of all, I pray they will have Your eyes and learn the wonders of Your ways.

Help me teach my children the lessons in Your Word. Remind me to talk about Your Scriptures in our home. May this become a way of life. Through the years, I pray my dear ones will learn to apply Your lessons to all they do.

When I must discipline, grant me love, strength, and consistency. Let me lead them into a life of love, responsibility, truth, and hope for the future. Grant me understanding as I work with each child, so I won't be too strict nor too lenient. Help me develop love and security in them, rather than fear and anger. Let everything I do be out of loving action, not reaction.

I can't think of a job more challenging than meeting the needs of my children. I can only do it through You, my Lord. Go before me, I pray. As I endeavor to do Your will, I petition Your help. Enable me to train up my children in the way they should go, so when they are older they will remain close to You. In Jesus' name I pray, Amen.

HURT FEELINGS

"But when you are praying, first forgive anyone you are holding a grudge against, so that your Father in heaven will forgive you your sins too."   MARK 11:25 TLB

Instead, be kind to each other, tenderhearted, forgiving one another, just as God has forgiven you because you belong to Christ.   EPHESIANS 4:32 TLB

Don't just pretend that you love others: really love them.   ROMANS 12:9 TLB

SEPARATE WAYS

Barney and Paul were good friends. Their close friendship made them like brothers. They went to church, prayed, and felt God call them to serve on the mission field together.

The two men's personalities were completely opposite, however. Barney had a loving, caring way, always trying to encourage people to seek God. Paul told people about Jesus with vigor and drive. He had total focus on the most efficient way he could spread the gospel to as many people as possible. Both men served God to the best of their abilities.

On one of their mission trips, Barney decided to bring his cousin Mark along. Partway through the trip, Mark told the two friends he wanted to go back home. Barney and Paul continued their work of winning souls for the Lord.

A new mission trip was planned. Barney wanted to continue encouraging Mark by bringing him along again. Paul reminded Barney how Mark had abandoned them before, and he gave a firm "No." Tempers rose. Harsh words were spoken. Barney and Paul decided to go their separate ways.

As you can probably tell by now, this modern-day story spins off from the Bible, telling about Paul, Barnabas, and Mark (Acts 15:36–41). Hurt feelings must have been deep.

None of us really know what God's will was for Paul or Barnabas. God certainly must have hurt for them. In spite of it all, God blessed each of their ministries. In time, their wounds healed.

Sometimes Christians disagree, many feeling they are led of God. After struggling to work things out, they give up and go their separate ways. They may try to make things right, but the hurts go too deep.

When this happens, our concerns must be brought to God and left for Him to handle. God can help us forgive, even if the other person isn't sorry. Not forgiving is destructive. When we allow Him, God creates a new work within us, making a pure heart, free from bitterness and acceptable to Him.

This can be done only when we call upon God for His power and love. We wait on God while He deals with our lives and the lives of those who hurt us. We realize we must change where we're wrong. We must forgive, let the faults of others go, and pray for these people. It may take time to heal. However, God has an amazing way of turning our bungles and poor attitudes around. He can do remarkable things in our lives.

In spite of everything, God has the love and compassion to bless those who long to serve Him. He works things out simultaneously for good in what is best for us and for others, when we obey Him. Paul later wrote, in Colossians 4:10 NIV: "My fellow prisoner Aristarchus sends you his greetings, as does Mark, the cousin of Barnabas. (You have received instructions about him; if he comes to you, welcome him.)"

I SURRENDER ALL

All to Jesus, I surrender;
Lord, I give myself to Thee;
Fill me with Thy love and power;
Let Thy blessing fall on me.
I surrender all, I surrender all,
All to Thee, my blessed Savior, I surrender all.

JUDSON WHEELER VAN DE VENTER, 1896

TAKE MY PRIDE AND PAIN

Father, You know how much I hurt right now. I tried to make things right, but people simply don't always agree. Help me to forgive, even when I feel others are wrong. Remove my stubborn pride, Lord. Heal my pain. Comfort and restore others who are hurting. Help me surrender all to You and not take back anything.

I may not be able to do anything else at this time to solve this problem, but I know You can. Please be with those from whom I am distant. Remove all grudges, I pray. Bless and surround us with Your cleansing, forgiving Spirit. Grant us help to love and overlook the past as we press forward with You.

SHAKING THE HABIT

"If you hold to my teaching, you are really my disciples. Then you will know the truth, and the truth will set you free." JOHN 8:31–32 NIV

For you did not receive a spirit that makes you a slave again to fear, but you received the Spirit of sonship. And by him we cry, "Abba, Father." ROMANS 8:15 NIV

"So if the Son sets you free, you will be free indeed."   JOHN 8:36 NIV

GIVING HABITS TO GOD

Jeremy, Cheryl, and their older children loved watching their curly-headed little girl, Talia. Everything she did was cute. They recognized, however, that Talia wasn't a baby any more.

Everyone knew Talia loved her binkie and blankie. She carried them everywhere. If the family went to the store, they waited while Talia dragged her blankie out the door to the car. She was often asked to remove her binkie while she talked, so people could understand her. Once the blankie got caught in a grocery store automatic door. Jeremy and Cheryl frantically dislodged it before someone tripped.

The time had come for Talia to break the habit of depending on her two favorite things. Jeremy and Cheryl tried reasoning with Talia to give them up, with no success. Talia's curly head bounced, her lower lip jutted out at the very mention of relinquishing her comforting habits.

After much persuasion, though, they finally succeeded, and Talia was free to move on to more grown-up interests. We all have habits, some good, some bad. We may like to read the Saturday paper. We sit in the same church pew every Sunday morning. We drive the same streets to the store. We may love to sing in the shower. We plant kisses on our loved ones every morning and have a habit of praying together before we go about our days.

Some habits are fine. However, other behaviors can ruin our lives. Those who love us may even have to suffer. Our children often copy our example, whether we want them to or not.

What we allow to go into or come out of our mouths is habit-forming. Our routine attitudes and body language form our character. What we read, listen to, or watch on TV become habits and show up in our behavior. They can make or destroy us.

Like Talia, these habits are sometimes too difficult to break on our own. We can get help to shake them from instruction books, doctors, counselors, and friends.

But the greatest helper of all is our heavenly Father. As we give our negative habits over to Him, He provides the strength for us to shake them. We can let go of these childish things and be set free to enjoy a healthy, victorious life in the Lord.

HE IS JUST THE SAME TODAY

Is it true that ev'ry sickness
May be laid at Jesus' feet?
All my trouble, care, and sorrow,
And I rest in joy complete?
Yes, my friend, in ev'ry sadness,
If by faith to Him you pray,
He'll remove with tender mercy,
For He's just the same today.

JACOB W. BYERS, 1897

FREEDOM

Father, thank You for helping me break this terrible habit. It is no longer my habit, because I've given it to You. Thank You for how each time I'm tempted to pick up that crutch again, You give me the strength to firmly say, "No!" I'm excited about the freedom You have given me, because I am no longer bound by this awful habit. Thank You for breaking the bonds that once bound me to it. Now I'm filled with joy and gladness in You, Lord Jesus, and have a new, victorious life.

Each day, I commit my free life to You. Help me, I pray, to deliberately turn my back on any temptation and not reconsider it. Thank You for giving me strength and victory. I give You all the praise and glory for setting me free!

For His
Name's Sake

BEING A CAREGIVER

Let us not become weary in doing good, for at the proper time we will reap a harvest if we do not give up. GALATIANS 6:9 NIV

CARING ENOUGH TO GIVE

Kammy heard a siren and glanced out her living room window in time to see an ambulance pull in front of Ellen and George's house across the street. She and the children ran to the front yard fence, wondering what was wrong.

Kammy knew her neighbors were getting up in years, so she said a silent prayer for their health. After what seemed like hours, Kammy could see the paramedics carry Ellen out of the house on a stretcher, then carefully lift her into the waiting ambulance. The ambulance drove away, with George following in his car.

The family kept checking George and Ellen's driveway throughout the evening. George finally arrived. Alone. Kammy felt cold chills. Her husband Darren hurried to George and invited him over for a cup of tea.

The three sat around the kitchen table, the children clustered near George's chair. No one knew what to say.

George buried his head in his hands. "Ellen had a stroke." His words were muffled. "The doctors said she'll be in the hospital for awhile, but will need a lot of help when she comes home." He raised his head, and his eyes brimmed with tears. "We have no children. You are our dearest friends."

Kammy squeezed George's hand.

"It's going to be all right," Darren reassured. "We're here for you."

The children clung to George and patted his arms and back. "We love you, Uncle George. Don't cry."

During the next few days Kammy cooked casseroles for George and often had him over for dinner. Darren watered George and Ellen's yard while the older man kept a steady run back and forth to the hospital. Darren, Kammy, and the kids took flowers up to Ellen as soon as she could receive visitors.

After Ellen returned home, Darren and Kammy realized that huge responsibilities would be required in helping Ellen recover. Kammy watched as various nurses and therapists bustled in and out of the home. She noticed the drawn look on George's face. Being a caregiver was taking its toll.

Darren and Kammy formed a plan. Darren would help George with the yard work and take the older man out once a week for lunch and a round of golf. While they were gone, Kammy would clean the elderly couple's house. She cooked some meals that would be easy to freeze and reheat. The children wanted to read to Ellen and visit with her, when she felt up to it. On Sundays, the family members would take turns staying with Ellen so George could go to church.

Ellen gradually recovered. She was able to do almost as much as before her stroke. Through it all, the two families drew closer than ever. Darren and George continued their lunch and golf dates. Kammy and Ellen helped each other around their homes and went out to lunch and shopping with the children.

Darren and Kammy thank God for how He made all of their lives richer, because He taught them how to care enough to give.

O PERFECT LOVE

Grant them the joy which brightens earthly
    sorrow;
Grant them the peace which calms all earthly
    strife,
And to life's day the glorious unknown morrow
That dawns upon eternal love and life.

DOROTHY BLOMFIELD GURNEY, 1883

LIGHTENING THE LOAD

Lord, my friend is weary caring for her loved one. Show me how I can help, without intruding. Though my time is limited, teach me how to gauge my day so I can reach out and care, if only with little things. I realize if I give a cup of water, I'm aiding this dear one like I would You.

Let me do it with love, not expecting anything in return. Let me give with a joyful, willing heart. Most of all, I pray Your love will overflow to my friend and the one she cares for.

UNANSWERED PRAYER

I waited patiently for the LORD; he turned to me and heard my cry. He lifted me out of the slimy pit, out of the mud and mire; he set my feet on a rock and gave me a firm place to stand.   PSALM 40:1–2 NIV

GOD'S BETTER ANSWER

Ian hung up the phone and shouted a triumphant "Yes!" Only twenty-three years old, he felt proud to have earned a degree in marketing from a local college. The icing on the cake was the phone call.

For several months, Ian had prayed for a successful marketing position. He felt God wanted him to put out his best, and a high-paying job would certainly bring a good tithe toward God's work. He sent out résumés all over the country. If he left his hometown in Washington, Mom and Dad would understand.

The phone call affirmed Ian's answer to prayer. A marketing position in New York opened up. He was to start in two weeks with a high-paying salary and benefits. No doubt, this must be God's will. Ian's feet barely touched the ground for the next few days as he prepared for the move to New York. His parents and friends appeared happy for him, but he would truly miss them.

A few days after the New York phone conversation, another call came. It was the company in New York again. Sincere apologies were given as the person on the other end of the line gave Ian some bad news. They would not need Ian for the job position after all. They had found someone more qualified to meet their needs.

Ian hung up the receiver and slumped into a chair. What had happened? He thought his prayer was being answered. He didn't understand.

Soon after, Ian found a different job as an assistant manager for a local department store. He dedicated himself to his work. Deep inside, however, Ian felt like God had let him down. He couldn't forget the dangling carrot of the New York job. He felt like a failure.

To keep his parents happy, Ian kept going to church. Good friends tried to console him with little success. Little success, that is, until an older man in the church recognized Ian's needs.

The man walked over to where Ian remained after a regular morning worship service and sat down beside him. The man reached over and put a hand on Ian's shoulder. "Ian, I believe God did answer your prayer, only the answer was a firm 'No.' You're not a failure. You are sharp and talented. God knows your needs and has something far better planned for you. Go home and read Romans 8:28."

The two prayed together. A peace Ian hadn't felt for a long time came over him. He decided to not dwell on the past. He would press forward and focus on what God wanted him to do.

Several years later, Ian and his wife, Melissa, sat together on the lawn swing. Ian was thankful he had remained in town. If he hadn't, he wouldn't have met Melissa. He felt completely fulfilled as he watched his loving wife at his side, his father playing catch with their two sons, and his mother holding their little girl.

Ian was now general manager of several stores, making it possible for Melissa to work part-time at the hospital and be home more.

Ian hugged his wife's shoulders. He thought about God's blessings over the years. More than ever, he thanked God for saying no to his prayer many years ago and giving him a better answer.

FULLY TRUSTING

All my fears I give to Jesus!
Rests my weary soul on Him;
Though my way be hid in darkness,
Never can His light grow dim.
All I am I give to Jesus!
All my body, all my soul,
All I have, and all I hope for,
While eternal ages roll.

J. C. MORGAN, LATE 1800s

I WILL WAIT ON YOU

Lord Jesus, I wait for You to answer my prayer. The time seems an eternity. I love You and strive to do Your will. Must it take so long?

Grant me patience, I pray, for I realize Your timing and wisdom are perfect. You know my prayer before I ask. I believe You have already brought it to

Your Father in heaven on my behalf.

I trust You and will not fear as You determine the best way to answer my prayer. I leave my request at Your feet and will rest in Your constant love and care.

Yea,
Though I
Walk Through
the Valley of
the Shadow
of Death

DEATH

*But our citizenship is in heaven. And we eagerly
await a Savior from there, the Lord Jesus
Christ, who, by the power that enables him to
bring everything under his control, will trans-
form our lowly bodies so that they will be like his
glorious body.* PHILIPPIANS 3:20–21 NIV

BEGINNING A NEW LIFE

From the moment we draw our first breath as babies,
we have a God-given determination to make these
mortal bodies of ours live, grow, and thrive. Life is
precious. We want to hang onto it for all we're worth,
and we seldom desire to give up this earthly world
we know.

When we are about to die, however, I believe
God will be with us every step of the way through
the valley of death.

It is interesting to note that some refer to the
Kidron Valley, located on Jerusalem's northeastern
slope, as the valley of death. During winter, Kidron
Valley floods with deadly torrents from underground
water. In summer, it is dry and unbearably hot. Its
steep, naked banks hug dreary burial grounds no one
has ever wanted to walk through. When Jesus left
Jerusalem on the night of His betrayal, He might

have crossed the northern end of the Kidron Valley to reach the Garden of Gethsemane. But those brave enough to walk the twenty miles south to the other end of the valley find the Spring of Gihon filled with pure, sweet water.

When we are about to leave this world and approach the valley of death, we need not fear. Jesus has gone before us. He will be there, ready to take our hands and safely lead us through to His living water and life eternal. These frail bodies we've hung onto so tightly will no longer matter. In light of His glory, we'll shed our mortal shells and realize we aren't dead at all. We shall have new lives that will never end. We won't feel sickness or pain. Sadness and tears will be no more. We shall begin a brand new life of joy and peace. We will become complete with indescribable blessings from our Lord.

THE SANDS OF TIME ARE SINKING

The sands of time are sinking, the dawn of
    heaven breaks;
The summer morn I've sighed for—the fair,
    sweet morn awakes:
Dark, dark hath been the midnight,
    but dayspring is at hand,
And glory, glory dwelleth in Immanuel's land.

ANNE ROSS CUNDELL COUSINS, 1857

Bring Me Home, Lord

My earthly time is ending, Lord. I say good-bye to my dear ones. Take my hand, I pray, and lead me on. I fix my thoughts on You as You carry and comfort me.

You assure me. I have no need to fear. Though death has its sting, so much greater is Your victory. You are my Conqueror and Deliverer. Your love surrounds me. Your Holy Spirit dwells within me. Your constant assurance removes my fear, for You are my mighty God.

Bring me home, Lord, so I can be with You. I will shed this aching body and take on a new life immortal. I grasp Your hand as we walk together into eternity. No tears will dim my eyes. I will no longer mourn or feel any pain. Old things in my life will pass away. Everything will become brand new, as You bring me home to meet our Father in heaven.

Grief

"Blessed are those who mourn, for they will be comforted." MATTHEW 5:4 NIV

But he was pierced for our transgressions, he was crushed for our iniquities; the punishment

that brought us peace was upon him, and by
his wounds we are healed. ISAIAH 53:5 NIV

LOSS

Numerous losses in our lives cause grief. Death of those we love is only one of many. Whatever our loss, whether it appears great or small to others, the ache and emptiness go deep. The pain can become unbearable.

Because we are Christians, we may want to believe God gives us the power and strength to skip over grieving like we would clear a hurdle. This may be true for some people, but I have never seen it happen.

Grief is a God-given tool to help us survive losses so great we can't handle them in one chunk. There seem to be no shortcuts. The steps taken in grief are like peeling an onion, one layer at a time. There are no rules, no timetables. We can't say we'll conquer grief like a cold or the flu. There is no comparison. Although comfort and love from others help, it is still a slow, steady process as we search our hearts and minds for answers.

The greatest consolation we have is God's promise of hope for the future. He shows a way through. I have been told in order to heal, we must allow ourselves room to grieve. Loss can be heartbreaking and disastrous. Grief is a necessary, restoring process.

Here are a few characteristics of grief I have gleaned from others and my own experiences. They may vary in order and circumstance. Through all of them, we can be assured God is with us.

- *Denial and isolation:* When first confronted with our loss, we don't want to believe it. "This can't be happening. Not to me." Denial acts like a buffer, allowing painful loss to sink in gradually. During this time, Jesus is with us, patiently waiting while we sort it all out. Little by little we turn to Him, then our family and friends for comfort and strength. (Read Deut. 33:27.)

- *Anger:* "Why me? Why now? I feel cheated." I believe the best thing to do during this time is for us to be open and tell the Lord exactly how we feel. God already knows us through and through, but we need to pour out our angry feelings to our Lord. Some of them may be accurate, some displaced. We may even become angry with Him, but God has broad shoulders. He is patient and understanding. We can spend hours telling Him our sorrows. He will never tire of listening. The more we share with Him through a journal or spoken prayer, the easier it will be for things to fall into place and the anger to burn out. (Read John 16:33.)

- *Bargaining:* Considering all the options and trying to find an easier way through are no strangers to us. We beg and argue with doctors, counselors, friends and family, ourselves, and God. There must be another or better answer. After we exhaust all possibilities, we at last turn to God for direction and strength. (Read John 14:1.)

- *Depression:* We feel abandoned and alone. No one seems to care or understand. Why should we care, either? At times we may not even feel the presence of God. Our prayers lie silent on our lips. But Jesus knows our hurts. At that very moment, He is bringing them to His Father in heaven. Imagine what Jesus went through at Gethsemane, or while He carried the cross and fell, or when He hung on the cross and heard the crying and jeers. Think how He bore our sins on His shoulders, the three days He lay in the tomb. Remember the timing of His glorious resurrection. Jesus carried His cross, but now He carries your cross and mine from darkness to light. (Read Matt. 11:28–30, Rom. 8:26.)

- *Acceptance:* Although we are deeply

saddened over our loss, God helps us find the way to accept. We wonder what our next step must be. When we cry out to Him again, God in His infinite wisdom and love reaches out and takes our hand, ready to lead us on.

- *Hope:* Jesus is our resurrection and life. Whatever our loss, He brings us through. He gives us help today and hope for tomorrow. There is no hopelessness in Christ. He has a way of providing us with a vision of what He has planned for our future: an abundant life in Christ Jesus. (Read John 10:10.)

HOW SWEET THE NAME OF JESUS SOUNDS

How sweet the Name of Jesus sounds
In a believer's ear!
It soothes his sorrows, heals his wounds,
And drives away his fear.
It makes the wounded spirit whole,
And calms the troubled breast;
'Tis manna to the hungry soul,
And to the weary, rest.

JOHN NEWTON, 1779

RETURN TO ME
YOUR GLADNESS AND JOY

My heart faints from all my grief, O Lord. How can I endure much more? Be merciful to me, I pray, and comfort me in my sorrows. My whole being is filled with agony, my soul overcome with distress.

I try everything to get past these sorrows. Nothing works. The comfort from those who care means so much—but it doesn't take away the pain. When I kept silent, my grief worsened. Day and night I cannot sleep. My strength is almost gone. I turn to You, Lord, and ask for You to deliver me. You are my Comforter, my Guide, my Healer. Return to me Your gladness and joy, Lord, as I put my trust in You. I praise You, my Lord, for walking this road of grief with me. Even when I feel alone, I know You are still here. Your hand lifts me up as You gently lead me through. Your healing balm soothes my soul. Your counsel and wisdom guide me.

Thank You for helping me see beyond the darkness and into the light. You give me hope for the present and vision for the future. Thank You for directing me to let go of the past and move forward with You. With joy and gladness, I praise You for all You do.

I Will Fear
No Evil

FEAR

*But You, O LORD, are a shield for me, My glory
and the One who lifts up my head. I cried to the
LORD with my voice, And He heard me from
His holy hill. I lay down and slept; I awoke, for
the LORD sustained me. I will not be afraid of
ten thousands of people Who have set themselves
against me all around.*

PSALM 3:3–6 NKJV

COMFORTING ARMS

Work on my busy night shift came to an end. I bid
everyone a good-night and glanced at the clock on
the way out the door. Almost one o'clock A.M. Going
home at last.

My muscles stiffened as I folded into my Toyota.
"Thank You, Lord, for my little car," I whispered.

In only a few minutes, I approached the turn to
our house. Lights were flashing everywhere from a
police roadblock. There must have been six patrol
cars surrounding the area, while a group of people
stood on the corner watching.

I made a U-turn and circled the block to reach
our home. Two more police cars parked on the corner near our house. My mind raced, and I whispered
another prayer. "Lord, could it be an accident? Is

anyone I know involved? I hope everyone is all right. Please help them."

While the questions flew through my mind, my curiosity took over common sense. The corner was only two houses away; the obstruction, one block down near the apartments, directly behind our backyard. I decided to walk down and peek around the corner. I would lock my car when I returned.

I was used to coming home from work in the middle of the night. My drives home were always cautious, but with almost no fear. "I can't believe I'm doing this," I mumbled. I ventured to the corner house, preparing to take a look, when a POP, POP, POP, POP filled my ears. It sounded like gunshots!

I never knew I could run so fast. I flew to my little unlocked car, scrambled in, slammed the lock down, and scrunched as low as I could. My heart was pounding. I wanted to be invisible. Why did the porch light have to be on? (Bless my husband's heart.) And why did it take thirty seconds for the dome light to turn off in the car *after* the door was closed?

I waited until the shots stopped, and then slipped out and locked my car as quietly as possible. I fumbled for the house key and entered our welcoming home. Curiosity spurred me on again, so I crept to our kitchen window, overlooking our backyard. POP, POP, POP! The shots seemed closer. This was too scary for me. I hustled down the hall to the bedroom and my sleeping husband.

POP, POP, POP, POP! The sound rang over our

back fence. Fear penetrated my whole being. How far could bullets fly?

Bob raised up in bed. "What was that?" he asked foggily. Bob could sleep through an earthquake.

"It's gunshots!" I whispered hoarsely. "Hit the deck! Keep your head down!" I dropped my purse and bag to the floor. With one great lunge, I dove for the bed and landed with a belly flop, hoping I'd miss Bob in the final thud.

"Dear God," I managed, "please help those people out there. Keep them safe." I clung to Bob and shivered with fright. He pulled the covers over me and wrapped me in his arms.

The shots lessened. Bob's breathing slowed to a steady rhythm. How could he sleep at a time like this? I lay under the covers, shoes and all, for at least an hour, huddled in Bob's arms. My shivering stopped. I waited and listened.

Silence. After a long while, I rose and tiptoed to the window again. I could still see flashing lights. They would be there for a long time. I felt God urging me to trust Him and let those in charge do the worrying. I finally listened to Him and felt a sense of relief as He calmed my fears. I prepared for bed and rested soundly, thankful for God, the police, and the sweet husband I love.

The next day the neighbors buzzed, although some hadn't even heard the commotion. The police had been called to a domestic dispute. The woman and her children were coaxed from the home and apartment, while neighbors were evacuated. The violent man remained inside, refusing to leave. Unsure if he was armed, the police shot tear gas into the apartment. That's what the popping noise was. (It certainly sounded like a lot of gunshots to me.) I thanked God for my answered prayer. No one was harmed.

How many times do we find ourselves full of fear, perhaps with good reason? Fear of danger, bad influences on our children, the unknown, the future. . . The list goes on.

Sometimes when all is going smoothly, we find ourselves saying, "This is too good to be true. What will happen next? What if. . . ? What if. . . ?"

We have a loving heavenly Father Who knows the future and cares for us. We have no guarantees about what will happen, but we do know He loves and watches out for us.

Like Bob did for me that frightening night, God envelops us in His big, strong arms where we'll be safe. He loves us and surrounds us with His protection. He wants our trust in Him in return. Instead of worrying and being afraid, He asks us to leave it with Him and those He assigns to help.

When we cling to Him, His comfort and assurance drive away our fears. Finally, through His tender coaxing, we rest and trust in Him.

SAFE IN THE ARMS OF JESUS

Safe in the arms of Jesus,
　　safe on His gentle breast,
There by His love o'ershaded, sweetly my soul
　　shall rest.

FRANCES JANE (FANNY) CROSBY, 1868

FACING MY FEARS

A gigantic fear looms over me with foreboding, cruel threats. The longer I cringe and shy away from it, the bigger the giant becomes. Before I know it, Lord, this monster obtrusively towers over me, and I feel helpless. I can't see over, under, around, or through it. It's just too big!

　　I find myself in this over my head. It is so frightening. I retreat to the safety of Your arms, Lord God, as You surround me with protection. Thank You for taking it over. I leave my plight to Your care and to those You placed in charge. Now I rest beneath Your sheltering wings.

DOUBT

*Then Jesus told him, "Because you have seen
me, you have believed; blessed are those who
have not seen and yet have believed."*

JOHN 20:29 NIV

STIRRINGS OF THE HEART

He showed a deep interest in Christianity as a child.
What he knew of God filled his soul to the brim.
He enjoyed listening to folks talk about the Bible's
teachings and hearing stories they knew so well.

Through the years, he sadly witnessed those
around him distance themselves from the Bible and
God. Fewer people knew the precious stories previ-
ously passed from one generation to the next.
Something was missing.

Now a young man, he saw the coolness and disre-
gard many showed to God and the Bible. It discouraged him greatly. Perhaps the lack of Christian
commitment caused him to doubt all he had learned,
and to simply believe in nothing.

Years later, though, a curious awakening stirred
within him. God finally got the man to reconsider
what he believed. The Bible stories he heard as a
child were coming to the forefront of his mind.
Again, he started asking if people could recall the

Bible lessons. Was there a God after all? Was Jesus Christ more than a man? Was He really the Son of God?

The man decided to see for himself. He took a trip to the Holy Land. There God stirred his heart. He returned home and began reading everything he could get his hands on by great theologians and religious leaders. He wanted to discover if the Bible was really true. He made a second trip to the Holy Land and learned more of its history.

At last, the man opened his mind and heart and allowed God to erase all doubt. He asked Jesus to enter his soul and replace his disbelief. A miraculous transformation took place in his life. He sought the advice of Christian leaders and set to work writing a story about the most powerful thirty-three-year life in history: the life of Jesus Christ. Fulton Ousler awakened and inspired the hearts of many and helped remove doubts about God when he gave the world his inspiring classics, *The Greatest Story Ever Told* and *The Greatest Book Ever Written.*

In spite of doubts and confusion that cloud our minds, God still ignites our hearts with the flame of love and trust. As much as in days of old, He overcomes adversity and affirms that *He is* our God. No doubt about it, God *is.*

When I Survey the Wondrous Cross

See from His head, His hands, His feet,
Sorrow and love flow mingled down!
Did e'er such love and sorrow meet,
Or thorns compose so rich a crown?

ISAAC WATTS, 1707

Praise Destroys the Doubts

Father, life is crushing in on me. I can scarcely feel Your presence. My mind whirls with jumbled thoughts: happy, sad, joyous, confused. Do You hear me? How might I feel Your needed presence? I understand You are here, but I don't always take time to heed Your presence. Please help me to do so. Instead of doubting, I will praise You for what You have already done.

Thank You for allowing me at any time, anywhere, the privilege of walking into the very holy of holies and communing with You. As we talk and I *listen*, You replace my doubt with Your encouraging presence.

OFFENSIVENESS

"But I say to you who hear: Love your ene-
mies, do good to those who hate you, bless those
who curse you, and pray for those who spite-
fully use you." LUKE 6:27–28 NKJV

THE DIFFERENCE IS LOVE

Many people are not accepted because they are considered different. The story of one little girl's love and
determination rocked the world and still softens hearts
today.

She was ridiculed and treated badly because of
her race. One day before her scoffers, she stopped and
prayed. She asked God to forgive the ones who mis-
treated her. She said even when they spoke badly
about her, the people didn't realize what they were
doing. Then little Ruby Ridges prayed again for God
to forgive them like He forgave folks years before who
said terrible things about His Son.

HE GIVETH MORE GRACE

His love has no limit; His grace has no measure;
His power has no boundary known unto men.
For out of His infinite riches in Jesus,
He giveth, and giveth, and giveth again!

ANNIE JOHNSON FLINT, 1862–1932

TEACH ME SELF-CONTROL

Father, thank You for teaching me to think before I speak or act. I know sometimes it's difficult for You to get me to listen. I praise You for how Your Holy Spirit warns me against serious mistakes. The words in Your Bible grant me wisdom and remind me to exercise self-control. May everything I say and do show kindness and love to others.

TEMPTATION

Let your eyes look straight ahead, fix your gaze directly before you. Make level paths for your feet and take only ways that are firm. Do not swerve to the right or the left; keep your foot from evil. PROVERBS 4:25–27 NIV

Looking Straight Ahead

My husband, Bob, recently took up walking three miles every other day in order to lose some weight and shape up. I decided several weeks later to join him on his walk through town.

While we trekked down Main Street, Bob shared a valuable lesson with me. He said walking was not the hard part. The challenge was passing the pizza shop, a hot dog stand, the doughnut store, two deli shops, and an ice cream parlor.

I thought a lot about Bob's story in relation to our walks with God. It isn't our step with God that's difficult, it's our walking (or running) straight forward, past the temptations along the way. We can do so only by focusing on Him.

Press On

Press on thro' strong temptation,
For Satan's hosts must flee;
In Jesus' name resist them
And vict'ry thine shall be.

B. ELLIOTT WARREN, 1897

I Focus on You

Though temptations surround me on every side, I keep my focus on You. I know You are far greater than any traps set in my way.

The devil often tempts me in my weakest areas. When this happens, I refuse to dwell on the temptation. Instead, I give the problem to You, Lord. Whatever temptations I face, others have encountered before me. I trust You to take them all, making a way for me to escape and be victorious in You.

Let me look directly ahead and focus on You, my Lord. Keep my way straight and level, my faith firmly planted in You. Thank You for leading and helping me every step of the way.

For You
Are with Me

BEYOND MY CONTROL

In the fear of the LORD there is strong confidence, And His children will have a place of refuge. The fear of the LORD is a fountain of life. PROVERBS 14:26–27 NKJV

READY TO BAIL

Raising a large family made it necessary at times for Bob to earn some extra money driving a truck. This time he was hauling a truck and trailer filled with nine thousand pounds of gasoline over Blewett Pass in midwinter weather.

Bob prayed with us for our safety and his, kissed us all good-bye, and was on his way. Having been dispatched in the evening, he would head over the pass, stay overnight, and return the next day.

The roads appeared clear as he started up into the mountains. Farther up, a little snow began to fall. There were no notices saying to put chains on the wheels, so Bob trusted the weather predictors.

As he continued climbing, snow accumulated to four or five inches. "Not bad," he said to himself, "but I'll keep the speed down."

A steep drop to the river lay at his right. Ahead stretched an abrupt incline. Bob coaxed the heavy gas-filled truck upward. By now, there was nowhere to turn around. "Almost to the top," he sighed.

Without warning, his truck wheels started to spin and lose traction. The truck and trailer came to a stop and then began sliding backwards. The cliff on his right now dropped about two hundred feet with no guardrail. The trailer jackknifed and slid directly toward the highway's edge. Saving the truck seemed hopeless.

Bob had the driver's door open, preparing to bail as he made a last-ditch effort to bring the truck back into control. If it continued to slide, the gas-filled giant would crash to the river hundreds of feet below and probably explode.

"Lord, help me!" he gasped.

Within seconds and for no apparent or logical reason, the truck regained traction and straightened itself out.

When he reached the summit, Bob thanked God for watching over him. He completed his journey on faith and a prayer.

During his trucking years, Bob had many other close calls. At times, everything seemed hopeless. We look back now and thank God for answering our prayers and bringing Bob safely home.

WHAT GOD HATH PROMISED

God hath not promised smooth roads and wide,
Swift, easy travel, needing no guide;

Never a mountain rocky and steep,
Never a river turbid and deep.
But God hath promised strength for the day,
Rest for the labor, light for the way,
Grace for the trials, help from above,
Unfailing sympathy, undying love.

ANNIE JOHNSON FLINT, 1919

TAKE THE CONTROLS, LORD

Life is out of control right now, Lord. Things are pretty frightening. I want to panic and bail out. Instead, I call on Your help.

Take the controls of my life, Lord. You can change chaos and fear into Your divine order. In quietness and confidence, I draw my strength from You. As You take the controls, I will rest and trust in Your wisdom and mighty power to guide me through.

MORE THAN I CAN BEAR

*Dear friends, do not be surprised at the
painful trial you are suffering, as though
something strange were happening to you. But*

rejoice that you participate in the sufferings of Christ, so that you may be overjoyed when his glory is revealed. 1 PETER 4:12–13 NIV

JESUS BEARS IT ALL

Are you facing troubles so difficult you feel one tiny straw more added to your load could cause you to break? Do you find no matter which way you turn, there is no escape and the walls of tragedy are closing in? Tell it to Jesus.

When you bolster all your strength and courage and try to carry the load, do you succumb to it instead and crumble beneath the weight? Tell it to Jesus.

Think of how Jesus carried the cross and took upon His shoulders the burdens of all humankind. Jesus didn't remain under that load. He went miles beyond the cross. By dying and rising from the grave, He set us free from all this.

He invites us to take His yoke upon us so He can make our burdens light. When we do this, we allow Him to help shoulder our load. Before long, we learn to synchronize our actions and motives within His will. The massive burdens may not lift right away, but be assured Jesus is near. In the same way He carried His cross, He helps us carry our loads today.

LEAVE IT THERE

Leave it there, leave it there,
Take your burden to the Lord and leave it there.
If you trust and never doubt,
He will surely bring you out.
Take your burden to the Lord and leave it there.

CHARLES A. TINDLEY, 1916

MAKE MY BURDENS YOURS, LORD

These burdens I carry are too heavy for me to handle any longer, Lord. I am going to break under the load. Shoulder them with me, I pray. Make my burdens Yours.

I don't have to worry about giving You a load that's too heavy. You, Lord, are greater than all. Now I wholeheartedly give You this burden and thank You. I already feel relieved, as though hundreds of pounds have been removed from my shoulders.

Your Rod
and Your Staff,
They Comfort Me

REJECTION

*"And whoever welcomes a little child like this
in my name welcomes me."*

MATTHEW 18:5 NIV

BEAUTIFUL EYES

Harrison and Linda decided to go out for dinner at a local restaurant. When they arrived, Harrison gave his name to the hostess and they looked around for a place to sit in the lobby. Harrison saw two empty seats across the room next to a mother cradling a little boy on her lap. He couldn't help noticing people turning away from the mother and child. When the couple came closer, they saw why.

The child had a growth on his face and a large birthmark. After he and Linda sat down, Harrison looked at the boy and smiled. In a flash, the youngster responded with a wide grin. His mother appeared pleased at the kindness shown. Harrison gazed into the most beautiful clear blue eyes he had ever seen. "Hi, I'm Harrison. What's your name?"

"Gabriel. Mama tells me I'm her little angel. She says I can sing like one, too."

Harrison and Linda were surprised at Gabriel's being so open. "Is it all right if he sings a song for us?" ventured Harrison.

Gabriel's mother nodded apprehensively but Gabriel enthusiastically belted out his first song. The little boy's voice rang out one tune after another while his mother held him close.

"Jesus loves me! this I know. . . ," "This little light of mine, I'm gonna let it shine. . . ."

Passersby stopped to listen. After Gabriel finished singing, the gathering crowd cheered and applauded. Some had tears in their eyes.

The hostess worked her way through the people and ushered mother and child to their table. The mother smiled at Harrison and Linda. "Thank you for caring," she whispered.

"Bye, Harrison!" Gabriel waved over his mother's shoulder to his new friends. "God bless you."

Harrison spoke softly in a grateful tone to Linda. "He already has blessed us—through Gabriel."

The next time you see someone who is disabled, don't be afraid to look him or her in the eyes and give a big smile. Even a "hi" would be good. When you do, you have done it as you would to Jesus.

JUST A LITTLE SMILE FOR JESUS

Just a little smile for Jesus,
Someone else may catch its ray,
Then another and another,
Till bright smiles have filled the day.

JESSIE KLEEBERGER, 1927

REMIND ME TO PASS A SMILE

I just came by someone who is disabled, Lord. Thank You for reminding me to pass a smile. Along with this, I pray Your blessings be upon this one.

Each dear child and adult is precious to You, just like me. Let lots of smiles pass their way, I pray. Help each person feel important and loved.

Thank You, Lord, for making my life richer; because when I pass a smile, they sometimes give one back to me.

DIVORCE

O LORD, when you favored me, you made my mountain stand firm.   PSALM 30:7 NIV

WORTHINESS FROM JESUS*

Final arrangements were made for Charlene's tragic, unwanted divorce. After her meeting in the lawyer's office, realization hit her with a devastating blow. She reeled from emotional pain as she drove her daughter, Jessie, to a routine eye doctor's appointment.

"Jessie, I'll sign in at the desk and wait for you in

the car." Charlene felt like her words weren't even coming from her mouth but from somewhere in the air. Jessie hugged her mom, silently left the car, and entered the office. Charlene leaned her head against the car window and closed her eyes. Gloomy thoughts filled her mind. It must all be her fault. She felt she wasn't worthy of love, not from her husband, not her children, not even God. How could she be worth anything to anyone?

A holy presence jerked Charlene out of her ruinous stupor. She realized these degrading thoughts were not of God. He loved her. She was His child.

She sat up straight and began to cry out to God. She didn't care if anyone around her heard what she had to say. "Lord Jesus," she prayed haltingly, "take control of my mind and emotions. I don't want to be destroyed by all these terrible thoughts. They are not of You."

She prayed for a long time, asking for God's forgiveness and help. She sought help to forgive and prayed for God to guide and encourage her husband, though he loved her no more.

Charlene felt God's presence surround her like a soft, warm breeze. She looked up and noticed a huge cedar tree towering proudly above the doctor's office. Its strong branches spread protectively over its surroundings.

"Jesus, that tree has weathered all kinds of storms." Charlene's voice lowered to a whisper. "Here it is, firmly rooted in the center of the city. Trees around it have been cut down. It's a survivor.

"I want to be like that, Lord. I have my roots sunk deeply in You. I know You are supporting me. I can stand tall in the midst of what my children and I are going through.

"I feel rejected and unloved right now. Still, I know You love me and are helping me overcome my distress. With You near, I'll grow stronger every day.

"Grant me strength to stand tall like this cedar tree. Give me enough wisdom and grace to be a blessing to those I love."

An amazing peace enveloped Charlene. She rediscovered the unconditional love and understanding Jesus had for her. Because of God's forgiving mercy, she was worthy of His love, and she knew He would lead her through.

*Names have been changed for privacy.
Written by permission from "CHARLENE"

WOUNDED FOR ME

Living for me, living for me,
Up in the skies He is living for me;
Daily He's pleading and praying for me,
All because Jesus is living for me.

GLADYS WESCOTT ROBERTS, b. 1888

Thank You for
Your Healing Process

Lord, this divorce is one of the most painful experiences I've ever been through. I don't think I can survive without Your understanding love.

It hurts so much, dear Lord. I feel like surgery is being done on me with a dull teaspoon.* My spouse has been a large part of my life. Now I'm losing that part of myself. Piece by piece is being cut away. Nothing is left of me. I feel I'm living a barren existence. I don't feel loved or beautiful anymore. Take my despondency and carry my grief, I pray. Replace my feeling of nothingness with Your blessed, holy presence. Be with and guide the one I love, also. You can go and help where I cannot. Thank You that through Your stripes, I am restored as Your healing process begins in me.

*Permission to use metaphor
given by a good friend.

Loneliness

He is a father to the fatherless; he gives justice to the widows, for he is holy. He gives families to the lonely. PSALM 68:5–6 TLB

PENNED FRIENDSHIP

After Shirley Green's husband died, she felt crushed and lonely. How could she manage? Shirley loved her grown children, but she needed friends, too. Now that she retired from teaching, what could she do? She asked God to give her direction and fill her loneliness.

One afternoon, Shirley routinely checked her mail. "Water bill. Light bill," she murmured. "Some friends I have."

Beneath junk mail and bills, however, Shirley found a pink envelope. The return address, New York City. She opened it curiously. "Dear Mrs. Green, I'm Jennifer McCallan. You were my third-grade teacher. I hope this letter reaches you.

"I live in Miami now and love my work as a model. I'm still not married, but I'm very happy. I have great friends and go to a wonderful church.

"You showed me through your life what it meant to be a Christian. I just want to thank you.

"Lately, I've been thinking of you and decided to write. Please write back when you can.

"Sincerely, Jennifer

"P.S. Could you ever come to Miami for a visit?"

Shirley felt like electricity went through the letter. Could this be her answered prayer? She wrote immediately and renewed their friendship. When Shirley added Jennifer's new address to her little book, she noticed lots of friends and family she could write to. After a short time, she had pen pals all over. Shirley's list grew and her loneliness disappeared.

She enjoyed visiting friends she had made, including Jennifer, throughout the United States and the world. When she was home, Shirley took as much pleasure entertaining her friends in return.

Her pen pal list mushroomed to over fifty, but writing letters caused carpal tunnel syndrome to develop in her hands. With help from her family, Shirley purchased an electric typewriter. Her next step may be a computer and E-mail. The awesome part of God's answer is how Shirley can fill other people's loneliness. She gives a listening ear and comfort to many people. I wonder what Shirley will do next?

WE GIVE THEE BUT THINE OWN

To comfort and to bless,
To find a balm for woe,
To tend the lone and fatherless
Is angels' work below.

WILLIAM WALSHAM HOW, 1864

LONELY NO LONGER

Father, I couldn't stand being lonely any longer. I felt like the walls were closing in on me. Thank You for helping me find a way to change all that.

You showed me how to reach out to others who are lonely, too. In so doing, I have fulfillment and happiness in my life, once again. Thank You, Lord, for teaching me how to be lonely no longer.

SUCCESS

"Give, and it will be given to you. A good measure, pressed down, shaken together and running over, will be poured into your lap. For with the measure you use, it will be measured to you." LUKE 6:38 NIV

A BETTER KIND OF SUCCESS

Keith and Connie were thrilled when they found out their best friends in college had moved back to town. They had gone to the same school, the same church, and had even become Christians together at a special revival meeting in their church. One night, however, the two couples met for dinner and discovered their lives were now totally different.

Skyler was a teacher, Pam, a librarian. They recently started volunteering as church youth counselors. The couple sounded thrilled as they told about kids becoming new Christians.

Keith had become a successful businessman, Connie a general manager for a major firm. Keith and Connie told about their successes. Wealth and prestige had become their main focus.

"We just celebrated our son Joey's fifth birthday. We're able to give him all he wants and more," Keith reported proudly. "It's taken long hours of work, but nothing can stop us now, right, honey?" Keith elbowed Connie with a playful nudge.

Connie nodded blandly. "We go to church, well, when we can with such a time crunch from our work and all," she added with a sigh. "But our goals for success are worth the sacrifice, right?"

Skyler and Pam listened intently. Keith could tell when his old friend had something on his mind. "What are you thinking, Skyler? Come on. Out with it."

Skyler searched Keith's eyes. "I don't know if I should ask you this."

"Fire away." Keith leaned back in his chair and propped one foot on his other knee.

"How does God fit into your plans? Is He calling you and Connie to bless and glorify Him in some way?" Keith nervously cleared his throat. Skyler went on. "Is there a way you can serve God through all He's giving you?"

"Well," Keith muttered. "I'm sure glad I'm not the rich young ruler and being asked to sell all my belongings and give them to the poor." He chuckled nervously. "I don't know if I could."

Skyler smiled. "I'm glad God has blessed you

with so much. I'll bet He has a wonderful plan for you. He'll show you what it is."

Keith didn't know what to say. Connie absent-mindedly stirred her cup of coffee, waiting for another refill. Keith didn't notice how tired and stressed she looked.

The couples parted with a commitment to meet Sunday for church. The sermon Sunday was, "Have You Lost Your First Love?" Keith didn't hear many of the words, though; he was too busy wrestling with where he and Connie stood with God. Had they lost their first love, their love for Christ? Did they let money, belongings, and prestige come ahead of Him in their lives?

After church, both families introduced their children to each other and went to Keith and Connie's home for dinner. After a lovely meal and a good visit, Keith went to his son's room to check on the children. Before he stepped through the door, Keith overheard Joey bragging about his expensive toys and criticizing kids who were poor. Keith could hear himself in his son's voice. "We're better," the son bragged, "because we're rich."

That night Keith and Connie discussed the sermon and their son's cutting comments. "Something is terribly wrong, Keith." Connie's hand trembled around her cup of coffee. A tear slid down her face. "I'm tired and stressed. Because of our schedules, we have little time even for our own son."

Keith put his arms around his wife. "Let's make some changes," he answered.

Several months later, Christmas was approaching. Keith and Connie had managed to cut back their working hours, so their Christmas spending would be less this year. Surprisingly, Joey didn't seem to mind. "Come on, Mom and Dad," Joey called happily. "Let's hurry and meet the kids at church. We're delivering gifts to the children's home." Joey paused and turned toward his dad and mom. "You know, I'm glad we can do something like this for Jesus' birthday; and those kids are nice." He skipped out the door.

Keith hugged Connie. "Our ideas of success have certainly changed. They're a lot better now. What means the most now is if we can give back to God part of what He's already given to us."

Connie hugged him back. Keith could see a joy in her face he hadn't seen for years.

TRUE SUCCESS

To laugh often and much, to win the respect of intelligent people and the affection of children; to earn the appreciation of honest critics and endure the betrayal of false friends; to appreciate beauty, to find the best in others; to leave the world a bit better, whether by a healthy child, a garden patch, or a redeemed social condition; that someone has breathed easier because you have lived. That is to have succeeded.

RALPH WALDO EMERSON

How Will I Be Remembered?

How will I be remembered, Father, when I am gone? Will people think of wealth or fame? I hope not.

I pray they will remember my love for You and others. That would be my greatest reward.

Failure

So do not fear, for I am with you; do not be dismayed, for I am your God. I will strengthen you and help you; I will uphold you with my righteous right hand. ISAIAH 41:10 NIV

Starting Over

As an artist, he earned a meager living selling his paintings. On the side, he invented a water pump for firemen and a machine to cut marble, but no one was interested. He painted the portrait of President Monroe and did another of the members of the House of Representatives and yet another of Lafayette. When he heard that four murals were to be painted for the U.S. Capitol's rotunda, he wanted desperately to be chosen as one of the artists—but he was not.

Through the years, however, he developed

another dream and was determined to make it succeed. After much work and many failures, he put his project to the test. He and his partners ran an announcement in the New York paper. They wrapped two miles of wire in cotton, tar, and rubber all by hand and rowed across New York harbor to lay the wire. Operators stood on opposite banks. Everything tested perfectly.

Early the next morning, fishermen accidentally cut the wire. He not only failed, but now he was labeled a liar and fraud. At fifty-one years of age, however, he received money to test his invention again. He and his partners had two months to lay a line between Baltimore, Maryland, and Washington, D.C.

Samuel Morse sat in a room of the U.S. Supreme Court building, surrounded by dignitaries and reporters. He began the coded message: "What hath God wrought!" Later the invention labeled Morse code and Morse telegraph was used around the world. Samuel Morse said many could have invented the telegraph and code, but God saw fit to use him in the right place at the right time.

END OF THE ROPE

Are you at the end of your rope,
Struggling with strife and pain?
Do you feel you can't hang on?
For whatever you might gain?

Do your sufferings overshadow
Everything that is good?
You'll find that at the end of the rope,
God provides all that's good.

Are you at the end of your rope
With a load you cannot bear?
No matter how hard you struggle or try,
Does nobody seem to care?

Do you beg for strength to hold on,
When your being aches with pain?
You'll find that at the end of the rope
God is waiting, once again.

There at the end of your rope,
You'll see God's work is best.
There you can learn His answers for life,
While letting Him work out the rest.

If your goals and dreams are changing,
Your heart and mind renewed,
You've found that at the end of the rope
God lovingly cares for you.

Lord, I've tried to make this project succeed, but no matter how hard I strive, it just doesn't work. All I experience is defeat. I thought I was doing right. I don't know the answers, but You do. Take my defeat and teach me through it. Help me to measure success by how fully I trust and obey Your will. Thank You for caring for me when I am down.

And the next time I succeed, help me remember to listen to You while I am up.

DISASTER

These sufferings of ours are for your benefit. And the more of you who are won to Christ, the more there are to thank him for his great kindness, and the more the Lord is glorified. That is why we never give up. Though our bodies are dying, our inner strength in the Lord is growing every day. These troubles and sufferings of ours are, after all, quite small and won't last very long. Yet this short time of distress will result in God's richest blessing upon us forever and ever!

2 CORINTHIANS 4:15–17 TLB

CATHY'S STORY*

For years Kent and Cathy Shoop loved singing about God's love in churches and meeting places throughout the country. Kent belted out a clear tenor and Cathy's soprano voice sounded like a bird set free.

A few years ago, God called the couple to pastor a church in Tacoma, Washington, about ninety miles from their home in Easton. Cathy worked as librarian and student activities advisor for a local school district, and they both loved their home nestled amongst the Cascade Mountain trees, so they decided to commute each weekend to the church congregation they also loved.

Each Friday night they packed and drove over the pass to their small apartment in Tacoma, where they held worship services, visited people, and entertained company. On Sunday afternoons they returned home to the weekly work routine. Kent and Cathy continued singing in churches and at special events. Kent accepted a position as chairman of all the denomination's Pacific Northwest churches. Filled with ambition, they loved being active.

One Tuesday morning in early November, Cathy dressed in full winter gear, including mittens and hat, and started out for an aerobics class at Roslyn Fitness Factory ten minutes from home. She would arrive by six thirty, work out, shower, and return to Easton in time for her workday.

Without warning, Cathy hit some black ice on

Bullfrog Bridge. The car went into a spin and struck the right railing. Then it pitched into the air and flew over the side, landing upside down on the riverbank below.

Cathy found herself sprawled flat on the ground near her crushed car. She wondered why she couldn't move. She didn't feel cold, but she attributed it to her warm clothing.

Cathy drifted in and out of consciousness. She wondered if anyone could see her below the bridge. Kent wouldn't even miss her for an hour, when she was due at school. Indescribable peace came over her. She felt completely removed from everything. As she lay on the bank, God's presence and glory filled and surrounded her. Cathy knew God was in control.

Forty-five minutes dragged by. A screech of tires and a crash rallied Cathy as another car spun out and lodged itself against the bridge's railing. Cathy heard another car pull up. Two doors slammed. People were talking! Cathy mustered all the strength she could and cried for help. Thank God, they heard her. Immediately, someone called for an ambulance on a cell phone.

Cathy learned later that Kent received a phone call from her school asking why she hadn't shown up for work. He left immediately, retracing Cathy's driving route. By the time he reached the bridge, she had already been transported to the emergency room. How frightening it must have been for him to see the demolished car!

The first thing Cathy saw when she came to in the emergency room was Kent's loving face, filled with fear and concern. Her heart went out to him. "I'm sorry, honey," she stammered. She continued reassuringly, "Kent, don't worry. God is so big and real. God is alive and good!"

Kent told Cathy he had called their grown children. Again, she was sorry. A helicopter emergency crew struggled to keep Cathy alive as they transported her to Seattle's Harborview Medical Center. Cathy had ruptured her spleen, punctured a lung, and suffered a compressed spinal cord. She didn't remember anything from entering the emergency room until after the first week in the hospital, where she teetered between life and death.

When she rallied, Cathy was told she was paralyzed from the chest down. God's presence continued to surround and strengthen her. She never felt angry about what happened.

The Scripture "Though He slay me, yet will I trust Him" (Job 13:15 NKJV) gave Cathy courage and strength. A huge drive grew within her to keep going. With her determination, and her family's love, she could do it. Most of all, Cathy knew God was helping her. Intense physical therapy began as she pushed herself forward. Her main focus was: "I can do all things through Christ who strengthens me" (Philippians 4:13 NKJV).

Five months after the accident, Cathy returned to school in her wheelchair as librarian and student activities advisor. Kent and Cathy continued pastoring the congregation in Tacoma, driving back and forth each weekend.

Cathy could see Kent's growing fatigue from juggling responsibilities, so she offered to help. She took on the district's bookkeeping job. For three years, Kent and Cathy struggled to carry their load, working night and day. Cathy kept thinking, "I can do all things. . . ."

Then she felt her energy level crash. Cathy found herself physically crumbling under the load. The words "I can" were beginning to backfire. God was trying to teach Cathy she could do all things *through Christ* as *He* strengthened her.

After much consideration and prayer, Kent and Cathy felt God leading them to pastor a church closer to home. The district work has now leveled off and Cathy is learning to pace herself in school, church, and district responsibilities. Hard-learned lessons have taught her to lean more on God. Daily growth in the Lord makes her feel cleansed and complete. Little events and material things are less important. Life and time to accomplish God's will are precious.

Amazingly, Kent and Cathy still give wonderful messages in song, testimony, and example for God.

*Written with permission from
Cathy Shoop

GREAT IS THY FAITHFULNESS

Great is Thy faithfulness!
Great is Thy faithfulness!
Morning by morning new mercies I see.
All I have needed Thy hand hath provided;
Great is Thy faithfulness, Lord, unto me!

THOMAS OBEDIAH CHISHOLM, 1923

BLESSINGS IN DISASTER

Dear Father, this awful thing that has happened is shocking. Although I'm in a fog, I feel You carrying me already. Thank You for doing so.

I'm not at all courageous on my own, Lord, but I know You are my right and left. You go before and behind me as I struggle to get through. Thank You for sending me people who help. I praise You for Your love and care and for never leaving nor forsaking me.

You Prepare
a Table
before Me

OPPORTUNITIES

Be eager to give them your very best. Serve them as you would Christ. Don't work hard only when your master is watching and then shirk when he isn't looking; work hard and with gladness all the time, as though working for Christ, doing the will of God with all your hearts. EPHESIANS 6:5–7 TLB

THE NEW JOB

Liza's promotion took her by surprise. She was dedicated to her work, but never worried about a job change. She always did her best and left the rest in God's hands.

She felt excited about her new opportunity. However, numerous questions whirred through Liza's head. Was she ready for it? Would her coworkers like and accept her? How should she dress?

On the morning of her new job, Liza sat on the edge of her bed and whispered a quick prayer. "Lord, thank You for providing me with this promotion. I'm excited about this opportunity, but I'm very nervous. Even though I have a lot of questions, You know the answers. Please help me. Grant me confidence and a quick-thinking mind." More relaxed, she slipped on a nice outfit and went to work.

Liza's transition to her new position went more than well. Her associates were warm and receptive. She was pleased to find a few Christians in the group.

That night Liza thanked God for helping her to trust Him as she continued her work with dedication and love. As she went to sleep, she mused, *God gives me opportunities for an abundant life. I can earn a living through the plenty I receive—or I can gain a life through the plenty I give.*

GIVE OF YOUR BEST TO THE MASTER

Give of your best to the Master;
Give of the strength of your youth.
Throw your soul's fresh, glowing ardor
Into the battle for truth.

HOWARD B. GROSE, 1851–1939

I WILL USE MY OPPORTUNITIES FOR YOU

Father, as I begin this new job, I pray for Your help. Remind me to respect those in charge. I want to wholeheartedly do my best, so I can feel satisfaction for a job well done. I will concentrate on pleasing

You, rather than trying to gain favor from those around me. When things get tense, help me to not grumble but have a good attitude.

Thank You for the opportunities You give me. May I, in turn, use them to be a blessing for You.

BLESSINGS

As for God, his way is perfect; the word of the LORD is flawless. He is a shield for all who take refuge in him. For who is God besides the LORD? PSALM 18:30–31 NIV

TWO LITTLE THINGS

July warm breezes stirred around me as I waited at the Columbus, Montana, bus stop with Dad and Uncle Russell. I had taken a break from writing *When I'm in His Presence* and driven with Dad to visit my aunt and uncle in Columbus.

We had a great visit, but the time had come for me to return home. I planned to leave Dad with his brother and wife so they could have more time together while I would take the bus back. I would travel from late afternoon to early the next morning to my destination in Seattle.

I knew I'd lose sleep. However, the bag slung over my shoulder reminded me of the quiet time I could use to edit my book's second draft. *Please, Lord,* I prayed silently, *I'm asking two little things. Could you give me a seat alone, so I can concentrate? And, although I love them, how about no crying babies? We're out in the middle of Big Sky country. There shouldn't be very many people. Thank You, Lord.*

Shortly before the bus arrived, a polite young man came to the stop, wearing a baseball cap, plaid shirt, and blue jeans. Cal was on summer break from college, heading for Missoula to paint his aunt's house.

He greeted me with a winning smile. "Maybe we can sit together on the bus."

I smiled back and gave a feeble nod.

The bus hissed to a stop. I hugged Dad and Uncle Russell good-bye and boarded behind Cal. As I glanced around, my heart sank. The bus was packed. Almost every row was filled.

Cal found a place near the back. A young woman invited me to sit by her a few rows ahead, and I gratefully accepted. Another young lady slept on both seats in front of us.

It's okay, God. At least there are no crying babies. You must have a plan. I trust You to meet my need.

I glanced at my new neighbor as the bus joggled out. "Hi, I'm Anita," I offered, shuffling my bag in place beneath my feet.

"I'm Crystal," she replied with a half smile.

I noticed a large plastic bag bulging on the floor

in front of her. "Where are you heading?"

"Missoula." She sounded unsure.

I pulled out my manuscript and began editing. After going through a few pages, I felt a nudge at my heart. *What's wrong? Is God trying to tell me something?*

Crystal stared out the window. Although young, she looked like she had seen some hard times. I felt God's nudge again. I tucked my manuscript away and struck up a conversation.

Crystal told me she was going to Missoula to make a fresh start. She knew no one there. The bus was due to arrive at about nine thirty that evening, and she needed to find a shelter before the doors closed for the night so she wouldn't be on the streets. Crystal was homeless. She had hitchhiked from New Jersey until someone bought her a bus ticket to Missoula.

When the bus stopped for a dinner break, I told Cal about Crystal.

Cal grinned. "Not a problem. My aunt is picking me up. She knows Missoula like the back of her hand."

While I was in Columbus, I had sold four of my books to a lady there. Now I felt God strangely directing me to give my tithe to Crystal.

Just then Crystal came to me and asked if I had a couple of dollars so she could buy some food. I handed her five instead, then introduced her to Cal. She thanked us for the help and went into the store for something to eat.

I turned to Cal. "What are you studying in college?"

"Computer technology. I'm also an artist and I love to write." A distant look came to his eyes.

"I write, too."

Cal and I discussed the possibility of his joining a writer's group while going to college. He inquired about my writing, and I told him about my books on prayer. He looked pleased.

God nudged me again. "Would you like to read one of my stories?"

His answer was an enthusiastic "Yes!"

We climbed back on the bus. I couldn't believe I was handing my story four rows back to a complete stranger. Yet I knew it was the right thing to do. I passed back "The Impossible Calling." It told about how I started writing and the struggles I went through to fulfill my calling.

Crystal found a vacant seat in the front, so we could both have some space. The bus lurched forward. I pulled out my manuscript again. Time stood still as we cruised down the road. Pages flew, and I was amazed at how quickly I finished my editing.

As I was about to put everything away, Cal stepped up and handed me the story. His face wore a serious expression. "I'm a Christian," he said. He didn't seem to care who heard him. "After reading this story, I know God wants me to write. I guess I've known it all along." He thanked me and returned to his seat.

About that time, the young lady in front of me awakened from her long nap. She must have heard Cal talking. She stretched, turned around, and greeted me like she already knew me.

"You're a Christian?" Her long red, curly hair tumbled over the back of her seat as she leaned toward me, her bright blue eyes shining.

"Yes, I am." By now I was beginning to wonder what in the world was happening on this trip.

Her name was Elaina. She was returning home to her husband in Spokane after visiting her parents in Montana. When she wasn't waving her hands while she talked, she wrapped her arms around the back of her seat to steady herself. Hardly taking a breath, she told about her life as a kindergarten teacher, her husband, and her parents.

I listened.

Her face saddened. During her visit with her parents, an old friend had called. Elaina described how her friend's marriage had ended and his estranged wife lost custody of their children because of alcohol and drugs.

I listened some more.

The night after their phone conversation, Elaina's friend had reluctantly left the children with their mother for only an hour. His former wife and her drunk boyfriend took the children for a ride. A head-on collision killed everyone in the car.

"Why do things happen that way?" Elaina's eyes filled with tears.

We talked a long time about God's loving ways of helping us through, when we call on Him. Finally, she ran out of words. We all settled in and slept. Crystal and Cal stepped off the bus in Missoula. Elaina met her husband in Spokane. I prayed for them all.

Through the rest of the trip, I slept restlessly, still thinking about how God more than answered my prayer for two little things. He had also made a way to help with some big needs.

Bob met me at the bus in Seattle. After a big hug, he helped me with my bags, and we walked toward our car.

"How was your trip, honey?" he inquired.

"Amazing," I answered. "Absolutely amazing."

TALK WITH US, LORD

Let this my every hour employ,
Till I Thy glory see;
Enter into my Master's joy,
And find my heaven in Thee.

CHARLES WESLEY, 1740

Lord, my list of things to be done is so long I can't see the end. Thank You for helping me to concentrate on what really matters.

Thank You for granting me Your blessing and taking care of the little and big things. I know I must work and meet my obligations, but I also understand You have concern about the needs of others, as well.

Please keep reminding me not to become bogged down with things I know You can handle, so I can be a better disciple for You.

> *Therefore, since we are surrounded by such a great cloud of witnesses, let us throw off everything that hinders and the sin that so easily entangles, and let us run with perseverance the race marked out for us.*   HEBREWS 12:1 NIV

Marriage

> *"A man must leave his father and mother when he marries, so that he can be perfectly joined to his wife, and the two shall be one."*
> EPHESIANS 5:31 TLB

WE DO

The church was packed with friends as the simple ceremony began. Bob and I stepped forward and faced Pastor Jerry Phillips. My father stood by my other side, and we were flanked by four young men. Our friend, Phil, sang a lovely song, then Bob and I sang to each other.

Bob and I gazed into each other's love-struck eyes as Pastor Jerry led us through our vows. I was thrilled to my toes. Two of the young men presented us with our rings. Bob and I exchanged our tokens of love.

Pastor Jerry reminded us of the sanctity of marriage. His words went deep into our hearts. Then came the part, "Who gives this woman to be married to this man?"

A deep, reverent, "We do," chorused from my father and our four grown sons. We paused and prayed, thanking God for the lifetime of marriage and family He has given us. Bob and I hugged and kissed at the end of renewing our vows in celebration of our fortieth wedding anniversary.

Forty years, and we love each other more than ever. He still looks at me with a sparkle in his eyes. He opens doors for me, rubs my back, and buys me flowers. My heart still goes pitter-patter when he enters a room. When we go somewhere together, I still dress to look my best for my sweetheart and friend.

Our anniversary was more than a celebration of forty years of marriage. It was a celebration of life in

Jesus Christ with the ones we love the most: each other, our sons, our daughters-in-love, our grand-children, our parents, our family of God. Most of all, we celebrated our love for the Lord, the Author and Finisher of it all.

BLEST BE THE TIE THAT BINDS

Before our Father's throne
We pour our ardent prayers;
Our fears, our hopes, our aims are one,
Our comforts and our cares.

JOHN FAWCETT, 1782

THANK YOU FOR THE ONE I MARRIED

Thank You for the one I married, Lord, for the blessings You have bestowed upon us. It seems like yesterday when we stood before an altar and promised our lives to one another. Where have the years gone?

Thank You for teaching us to love, forgive, and love again. You are the head of our home. As we draw close to You, we automatically are united as one. I'm grateful for the many times we have combined our prayers for wisdom, love, and guidance; I thank You, too, for our children and grandchildren, so dear. Thank You for being with us during the good times, and for helping us when we face trials. Whenever either of us went through changes, we fell in love with each other again and again.

Bless us through our remaining years, dear Lord. Remind us to continue fanning the flame of love in our marriage, so it will always burn brightly with warmth and strength. May we grow old together, I pray. May he always bring me flowers. May I always bring a sparkle to his eyes.

In the
Presence of
Mine Enemies

SAFETY FROM WRONGDOERS

God is our refuge and strength, A very present help in trouble. Therefore we will not fear.

PSALM 46:1–2 NKJV

TWICE DELAYED

The clock wearily ticked down the minutes to an exhausting 3:30 A.M. Another nine-hour shift at the fast food restaurant mercifully ended the second of my two jobs for the day. I could only think of sleep.

My coworker, Tammy, and I trudged across the store parking lot to our cars. One of us would wait for the other before leaving, for safety's sake. I climbed into my car and turned on the key. Nothing but an irritating grind. It took fifteen minutes of shuffling jumper cables and recharging the battery before we could leave.

"Lord, this is frustrating," I muttered. "I'm so tired. But thank You for helping me finally be on my way home."

Tammy and I were going the same direction for a few blocks. I followed her zippy little red car around the bends. We reached the stoplight at a major inter-section. Tammy made it through; I was caught on the red.

Right after Tammy went through the light, I

saw a swarm of police cars surround her in the middle of the street. Two police cars fell in behind her, lights flashing, sirens shrilling. They forced her off the street, then recognized her, and went on. (Many of the police ate at our fast food restaurant and knew our night crew.)

I watched Tammy pull out again and leave. I decided to take a different route and was relieved to reach my safe, warm home.

The next day we discovered there had been a double homicide in an apartment near the restaurant at the same time Tammy and I normally approached the intersection. The fugitive had escaped on foot and was running through the area where we had planned to drive. My car's stalling had kept us out of danger.

I apologized to God for my muttering and thanked Him for helping us run late.

He Holds My Hand

Dangers surround me and dark is the way,
But Jesus leadeth me.
He is my strength for the long weary day,
No matter what may be.

NORMAN J. CLAYTON, 1938

JOINING HANDS IN PRAYER

How routine it is, dear Lord, for our family to join hands and pray each morning. We ask for Your guidance and protection from iniquity and harm until we return home.

At day's end, I often look back in awe at how You repeatedly honor our brief, yet sincere prayers. I scurry through my duties, striving to meet time limits. I may forget how we prayed that morning until the blessings ring through loud and clear.

Forgive me, Lord, for my impatience. I'm forced to work overtime. The car stalls. I hit every stoplight. My knuckles turn white, gripping the steering wheel. The line is long at the store. Still You are with me.

I don't see all the puzzle pieces, I don't always realize how frequently You intervene and protect. Your miracles must be more than I can number.

Thank You, Lord, for watching over us and bringing each of us home safely, all in answer to our routine morning prayers.

ENEMIES AND FRIENDS

Who then can ever keep Christ's love from us? . . . I am convinced that nothing can ever separate us from his love. Death can't, and life

can't. The angels won't, and all the powers of
hell itself cannot keep God's love away.

ROMANS 8:35, 38 TLB

FREEDOM FULFILLED

She was born in 1820 on a plantation in Maryland to a family of slaves. At a young age, she felt strongly that no one should be a slave. Her desire for freedom increased daily.

By the time she turned six, the child put out more work than most children her age. Because of this, her master decided to sell her for the good price she could bring him. When he rode up to her on his horse to place her in back of him, she stood her ground and shouted, "No!" After he threatened to whip her, the little girl's mother told her to go.

"Stay strong, child. The Lord is with you."

For the next several years the girl labored for farmers' wives: sewing, cooking, and caring for babies. At the slightest thing wrong, she was whipped.

Some people felt they should kill their masters to become free. The girl believed that wasn't what God wanted her to do. Instead, she praised God in songs about Moses' freeing the Israelites from bondage in Egypt.

At age fifteen, she helped a slave escape. She was hit in the head by a heavy whip and lost consciousness; she remained unconscious for several days.

After she recovered, the teenage girl would fall asleep at a moment's notice, but she still did not lose her trust in God nor her vision for freedom.

Once in awhile she was loaned out to work for her previous master, where her father and mother still worked. She was now a young woman, and her father listened to her determination to be free. Whenever she could be with him, her father taught her survival skills about the outdoors.

At age twenty-four, she was allowed to marry a man who had been given his freedom. Sadly enough, he wouldn't listen to her dreams of freedom.

But God showed the young woman a plan when a white Quaker lady on a buggy waited for her at the edge of the woods. Quaker Christians believed slavery was wrong. The woman warned the young slave she was about to be taken from her husband and sold again. The Christian lady helped set her on an escape route through the Underground Railroad to freedom.

With a little food in a cloth bag tied around her waist, she walked from one station to the next, through swamps, brush, and woods. She seldom slept. All she had to do was follow the North Star. Quaker families helped along her way, providing her with rest, food, and warm clothing, accompanied by their prayers. At last she made it to freedom. Altogether she had walked about 140 miles.

Even though she was safe, she chose to return and lead other slaves to freedom. Many called her Moses, for like the biblical hero, she led people out of captivity.

A reward of forty thousand dollars was placed on her head, but she made nineteen trips to free slaves, including her own family. Her husband did not support her, though, and he married again. By the time she finished, she had freed over three hundred slaves. She loved the Lord with all her heart and obeyed His leading.

Eventually, Harriet Tubman and her family settled in Auburn, New York, as free people. She used the rest of her life to crusade for women's rights and start a home for needy people. Most of all, she never stopped singing and thanking God for Quaker friends who helped her fulfill her vision to be free.

O Master, Let Me Walk with Thee

O Master, let me walk with Thee,
In lowly paths of service free;
Tell me Thy secret; help me bear
The strain of toil, the fret of care.
Help me the slow of heart to move
By some clear, winning word of love;
Teach me the wayward feet to stay,
And guide them in the homeward way.
Teach me Thy patience; still with Thee
In closer, dearer company,
In work that keeps faith sweet and strong,
In trust that triumphs over wrong.

Washington Gladden, 1879

Thank You for My Friends

Father, thank You for my true friends. They are the kind of friends who are there for me when things are right or when they go wrong. Thank You for the times they have gone out on a limb, because they love and believe in me.

Help me, I pray, to be that kind of confidant, and not be afraid to courageously stand up for them in all kinds of circumstances.

You Anoint
My Head
with Oil

HOLY SPIRIT

And Jesus came to them and spake unto them,
saying, All authority hath been given unto me
in heaven and on earth. Go ye therefore, and
make disciples of all the nations, baptizing
them into the name of the Father and of the
Son and of the Holy Spirit: teaching them to
observe all things whatsoever I commanded
you: and lo, I am with you always, even unto
the end of the world.

MATTHEW 28:18–20 ASV

GREAT AWAKENING

A young Presbyterian preacher clad in simple buck-skin rode his tired horse for hundreds of miles into Logen County, Kentucky. Armed with his treasured Bible and meager supplies, the fearless servant of God entered untamed territory where he met a mixture of people. Some truly loved the Lord, while others scoffed at both God and the laws of the late 1700s.

Rev. James McGready should have been fearful for his life in such rough territory. Instead, his plain-spoken ways and loving heart gained the trust of Christians and rebels alike. Wherever Rev. McGready went, he preached honest, easy to understand ser-mons. He described heaven and hell so vividly, those who listened either shouted for joy or trembled with fear.

Rev. McGready started three churches. "Prayer in faith believing" became his greatest strength and encouragement to keep going. As people accepted Christ, the young preacher charged them to pray for others. He encouraged them to ask God to pour out His Holy Spirit upon them and give the people a cleansing power.

Rev. McGready took his three congregations one step farther. He appealed to them to faithfully pray for others the night before and the morning of every worship service. He encouraged them not only to pray but also to fast, asking God to pour out His Holy Spirit and give the people a cleansing power.

It didn't happen right away, but after many months of prevailing in prayer, a revival began to break out. A new spiritual awakening was happening among his three congregations.

God's Holy Spirit swept through the church meetings like a mighty flood. Wave after wave of His powerful presence touched hearts and filled them with overwhelming blessings. God's power was almost more than they could endure.

Folks traveled hundreds of miles to attend the meetings. Before long the attendance reached into the hundreds. Other ministers came, and church denominations didn't matter. Several services took place at the same time in huge clearings, while many people camped there for days. Few wanted to leave as one revival after another came. Great spiritual awakenings had begun.

God raised up several dynamic long-remembered preachers because of these revivals. Their names and sermons still ring down through history: Francis Asbury, John Wesley, and Lyman Beecher were among them.

These courageous frontier preachers and circuit riders, along with many others, left the revival meetings and followed God's call. They loaded their Bibles and a few Christian books into their saddlebags and forged into miles of wilderness to reach those who hadn't come to the meetings.

The incredible part of the great spiritual awakening was it didn't end there. One example is shown in the life of the preacher, Lyman Beecher. God's Holy Spirit overflowed through his example to his children.

One generation later, in the 1800s, Lyman's son, Henry Ward Beecher, became a famous preacher, carrying Christ's great news throughout the English-speaking world. Well-known for his wisdom, he became a strong political leader for the Republican Party.

One of Lyman Beecher's daughters, Harriet Beecher Stowe, authored many inspiring poems and the classic novel *Uncle Tom's Cabin*. His son Edward Beecher wrote *Conflict of Ages*. Edward was known as a mighty wielder of the pen for God and humanity.

Numerous inspiring words have passed down

through generations of great leaders who were directly and indirectly affected by the Great Revivals. These timeless holy teachings still stir our hearts today.

Isn't it marvelous how all this began with the simple preaching and fervent prayers of one ordinary man dressed in buckskin, a man who was willing to be used by God?

FILL ME NOW

Hover o'er me, Holy Spirit,
Bathe my trembling heart and brow;
Fill me with Thy hallowed presence,
Come, O come and fill me now.
Thou canst fill me, gracious Spirit,
Though I cannot tell Thee how;
But I need Thee, greatly need Thee,
Come, O come and fill me now.
Cleanse and comfort, bless and save me,
Bathe, O bathe my heart and brow;
Thou art comforting and saving,
Thou art sweetly filling now.

ELWOOD HAINES STOKES, 1879

Here I stand, Lord. My kitchen sink may be my only altar, but You are so near to me I can nearly reach out and touch You.

Through the night and early morning I have sought Your direction. At this moment, You unexpectedly shower me with Your glorious love. Your awesome presence is almost too great to bear. I feel like I should remove my shoes, like Moses did; as though I am standing not on simple tile, but holy ground.

How can You be so wonderful, my Lord? All this time I have been pleading with You for my needs. You have taken them to Your Father, interceding on my behalf. Thank You.

Just as You prayed in the Garden of Gethsemane before dying for the sins of all humanity, You are taking my needs to the Father right now.

I praise You, Lord, that so many years ago You caused the thick curtain in the temple to rip from top to bottom, exposing the holy of holies to all who love and obey You. No longer are we separated from our Father's presence. Because of this, I can go right in and pour out my soul to You; any time, anywhere.

Remain with me, I pray. Linger with me just a little longer, so I may bask in Your warm, refreshing presence. Teach me what I must learn, and help me obey. Fill me to overflowing with Your Holy Spirit. Thank You for Your touch, Lord, for letting me stand on holy ground.

CALLED OF GOD

Now it is God who makes both us and you stand firm in Christ. He anointed us, set his seal of ownership on us, and put his Spirit in our hearts as a deposit, guaranteeing what is to come. 2 CORINTHIANS 1:21–22 NIV

THREE SOLDIERS' PRAYERS

Ben and Anna gave most of their lives to the ministry, serving faithfully as God's true Christian soldiers, loving and winning souls one at a time. Their congregations were never great in number. Their names didn't flash huge accomplishments in the church denomination newsletters. The couple simply kept plodding along, loving and serving the Lord.

After a while, though, Ben and Anna felt their energy start to droop. They knew they didn't have many more years to give to the same long hours of full-time Christian service. Was their work for God coming to an end?

Although they did their best throughout their ministry, Ben became filled with deep sorrow. He longed to have accomplished one great thing for God. This burden kept growing within him until he felt like a complete failure to God and to the people he tried to help. Anna could see the seriousness of Ben's despair.

No amount of comforting him could change the elderly minister's mind.

Finally, the two faithful Christian workers took the matter to God in sincere prayer. They asked Him for comfort and strength. Then they prayed for God to show them one significant thing they had accomplished that blessed the hearts of many.

Days, weeks, months passed. Retirement drew near. Ben and Anna's prayer life remained strong. The comfort and strength they asked for came, but not the answer to their second request. Were they wrong for praying in such a way? Could God be calling them to something new? Whatever God's answer was to their prayer and no matter how He led, Ben and Anna waited with peaceful hearts, ready to do His will.

Ben labored over his final message to his congregation. How could he say good-bye? Why was God laying the words on his heart for such a dynamic sermon to his small congregation? He knew better than to question. He would simply obey.

The final day of Ben's full-time ministry arrived. The church would have a reception after the morning worship service.

The organ began playing. Ben left his study and stepped to the pulpit. He was astonished. The sanctuary was packed! He gazed out over the congregation and recognized faces he hadn't seen in years.

Ben spoke the fiery message God placed on his heart: "Passing the Torch." Now he could understand why. Ben threw every ounce of strength into what

God wanted him to say.

The congregation laughed and cried with him. Many knelt in prayer at the conclusion of the service. One after another came to Ben and Anna during the reception and shared how through the years the couple's ministry had changed their lives.

One lady became a Christian doctor when everyone said she wasn't smart enough—everyone, that is, except Ben and Anna. A young couple who were in one of Ben and Anna's churches as teenagers were now about to leave for the mission field. A handsome, distinguished gentleman waited quietly until last.

When he stepped forward, Ben and Anna recognized Randy immediately. Could this be the scrawny, ill-clad, eight-year-old boy from Anna's church school class?

They had first met young Randy when they were pastoring a church five hundred miles from where they now ministered. His family never came to church. The father drank constantly. The mother worked many hours to make ends meet. The congregation had simply loved and nurtured Randy, whenever the boy had managed to get to church. Anna poured endless hours of spiritual nourishment and Bible verses into young Randy. One morning after class, the boy knelt with Anna and asked Jesus into his heart.

Not long after, without warning, Randy's family moved, leaving no forwarding address. The congregation was crushed at the thought of never seeing Randy again. In spite of this, Ben and Anna kept praying for Randy through the years. They knew God was able to make their prayers go where Ben and Anna couldn't.

Now the three embraced with tears of happiness. Randy told how he still kept Anna's teachings tucked in his heart. He never let the flame of hope go out.

The young man went to college on scholarships and grants and became a minister. He was currently pastoring a spiritually thriving church of two thousand only a few miles away. His voice held the same loving enthusiasm Ben and Anna once showed to him.

Randy had heard about Ben's ministry and retirement through some friends. Before that, neither knew the other was in the same area.

Randy's gaze met Ben's. "Pastor Ben, you and Anna are Christian soldiers that are too good to totally retire. I know God has a new calling for you." Randy took Ben's hand. "Would you be willing to come assist me in heading up our home Bible studies and evangelism ministry? I've been praying for some help, and I believe you and Anna are the answer to my prayers."

The retiring Christian soldiers returned home, thanking God not only for their two answered prayers, but for their new calling.

Where He Leads Me

I can hear my Saviour calling,
I can hear my Saviour calling,
I can hear my Saviour calling,
"Take thy cross and follow, follow Me."

Where He leads me I will follow,
Where He leads me I will follow,
Where He leads me I will follow,
I'll go with Him, all the way.

EDWARD W. BLANDY, 1890

Thank You for Calling Me

Though I don't feel I'm talented, thank You for calling me to work for You. I still know there are things I can do for You, Lord, and I am willing for You to use me.

I won't say, "I can't." Instead, I will be obedient to whatever You want me to do. Anoint me, fill me with Your power and strength, and use me for Your glory. In Jesus' name, I pray. Amen.

My Cup
Runs Over

GOD'S WARM PRESENCE

Oh, . . .give thanks to the LORD for His good-
ness, And for His wonderful works to the chil-
dren of men! For He satisfies the longing soul,
And fills the hungry soul with goodness.

PSALM 107:8–9 NKJV

CRAVINGS

It has been said we women have a vital need for a spe-
cific food element in our bodies: Chocolate! I like to
think this is true. When the pace picks up, stress
attacks, fatigue sets in. . .and chocolate calls, "Come
get me. Come get me." It just *has* to be a dietary need.

As each school year nears an end, teachers strip
the faculty room snack stand of its chocolate. When
deadlines approach, chocolate shows up everywhere.
I confess I like a nice cup of hot chocolate, especially
at the end of a long day. Its warm, smooth liquid
soothes and relaxes me.

Whether these things are good or bad remains to
be determined. However, we know that when our
bodies like something, our minds attempt to fit it into
our diets.

God gave us the greatest ingredient of all to meet
our needs: the warm presence of His Holy Spirit. As
Christians, our souls periodically become drained

and anemic. We grow weak and irritable. Before long, we crave precious time with the Lord, so we can be strengthened by His warm, calming presence.

God refreshes and rejuvenates us. His presence is more satisfying than a warm cup of hot chocolate or a good night's sleep. Our minds quicken, our emotions lift and remain intact as we drink in His presence.

It isn't like an instant fix. Seeking God's presence takes tuning in to Him with all our hearts, our souls, and our total beings. We must purposely put Him before everything else, in order to be honored with His wonderful presence.

And oh, when we have time with Him, it exceeds all else! Unlike our material solutions of hot chocolate or caffeine, which fade away, we have a holy God Who loves us every minute, every day. Whether we feel good or stressed, His presence meets and surpasses *all* our needs.

THE LORD'S MY SHEPHERD, I'LL NOT WANT

My table Thou hast furnished
    In presence of my foes;
My head Thou dost with oil anoint,
And my cup overflows.

SCOTTISH PSALTER, 1650

FILL MY CUP, DEAR LORD

In this quiet hour, I sit and talk with You, my Lord, about all the things in my life. You listen and love and care.

I seek guidance in Your Word as I prepare to embark on a new day. Fill my cup, dear Lord. Overflow my soul with Your warm, loving Spirit. Thank You for soothing and nourishing my thirsty soul.

UNLIMITED LOVE

"My command is this: Love each other as I have loved you. Greater love has no one than this, that he lay down his life for his friends.

"You did not choose me, but I chose you and appointed you to go and bear fruit—fruit that will last. Then the Father will give you whatever you ask in my name. This is my command: Love each other."

JOHN 15:12–13, 16–17 NIV

A tiny spark started the fire. In seconds it burst into a ceiling-high flame. In minutes, it slashed its destructive tongue throughout the old apartment building. Occupants escaped with only the clothing on their backs, frightened but grateful to be alive.

Multiple fire units arrived on the scene. Firemen dashed here and there hooking up hoses and setting extension ladders in place. Some checked to make sure all apartment dwellers were safe. After they accounted for every person, the entire building burst into flames.

Then people stared in disbelief. What was that coming out of a broken basement window? Everyone strained to see. A cat was carrying something. The frightened cat ran to a safe place at the base of a nearby tree. She gently lowered a kitten, eyes not even open yet, and looked up pleadingly at a lady nearby. Before anyone could say or do anything, the mother cat ran back into the window of the burning building. She brought out her babies one by one and laid them carefully together by the tree.

After a few trips, her hair grew singed, her face charred so badly she could no longer see. Every time she searched out a kitten and brought it to the tree, she touched each one with her nose, appearing to count them. Finally, she saved the last kitten and collapsed from exhaustion near her litter.

Paramedics kicked in to help the mother cat that

had demonstrated such love. Citizens did what they could. No one knew who the owner was, so mother and kittens were taken to a nearby animal shelter. Workers at the shelter took over, attempting to nurse the badly burned mother and her babies back to health. They kept her kittens close to increase her will to live.

The story hit the news. People called from miles around offering homes for the mother cat and her kittens. The mother cat lived and regained part of her eyesight. After a period of time, she and her kittens were all placed in affectionate homes.

The intense love this cat felt for her kittens compares to the kind of love we feel for those who are dearest to us. Many of us would give our lives to save any one of them. But as great as this love is, God's love goes way beyond all.

He allowed His Son to die for us so we could be free from sin and have eternal life. He follows and pleads with us to accept His gift so we can be saved. When we give our hearts to Him, we experience His unquenchable, everlasting love that is beyond compare.

Behold, What Love!

Behold, what love, what boundless love,
The Father hath bestowed on sinners lost,
That we should be
Now called the sons of God!

J. McGranahan, late 1800s

For Your Love,
I Praise You

How I praise You, Lord God, for Your unlimited, overflowing, perfect love. How good You are! You are my Lord of lords. You are my God. There is no other. No one else is above You!

In return, I love You more than all else. For Your love, I praise Your holy name. Amen.

Surely
Goodness
and Mercy
Shall Follow Me

IN SPITE OF. . .

God is our refuge and strength,
A very present help in trouble.
Therefore we will not fear.

PSALM 46:1–2 NKJV

GOD'S GOODNESS

It looked like a harmless bruise on Brad's leg, so he didn't think much about it. Being a father of four growing children, Brad often pushed his own aches and pains out of his mind. After all, his wife, Carrie, and the children were most important.

Brad went on to work, but by the end of the day, the discomfort in his leg was difficult to ignore. Still, he determined it would get better on its own.

The next morning Brad awakened to prepare for work. The bruise had grown to an alarming hard, red-hot area and doubled in size. Brad stood up by the bed and nearly collapsed from pain and sudden weakness.

When Carrie saw his leg, she became alarmed. "Brad, you must go to the doctor immediately," she insisted. "This is serious and should not be messed with."

No excuses or arguments from Brad would change Carrie's mind. He drove to the doctor and stumbled into the office. When the doctor examined him, Brad was shocked to see the spot still growing and a red streak working its way up his thigh. The doctor ordered Brad to go immediately to the hospital.

Brad and Carrie couldn't find a sitter, so Carrie remained home with the children. Brad asked God for strength as he made the half-hour drive to the hospital. When he arrived at the emergency room, Brad was promptly admitted.

Brad was glad now that Carrie had insisted he get medical help. He knew she was already contacting family and friends for prayer on his behalf. Meanwhile, though, he was so weak he could barely sit up in bed or talk on the phone. He knew his wife and family were worried, but he also trusted God and his family doctor to help him.

Several days went by. The threatening redness continued growing, slowly edging its way toward Brad's abdomen and vital organs. Would he lose his leg or even his life from this? He refused to harbor such a thought and kept trusting.

Huge amounts of antibiotics were pumped into his veins. Carrie lived on the phone and took the children every day to see their daddy. Brad's parents, brothers, and sisters hovered near. Everyone kept praying.

Tests results finally came back. Brad was fighting a bacterial infection. It had worked its way into his body through a hair follicle on his leg. Such an occurrence was extremely rare, but that didn't make the situation any less scary.

It took a week more for Brad to take a turn for the better. The doctors said Carrie's quick actions and accurate help from the medical team prevented the infection from developing into a fast flesh-eating disease. Had he waited one more day to see the doctor, Brad might have lost his leg and the infection could have gone to his vital organs.

Brad is amazingly well and hardy now. Everyone around him is surprised at how he regained his strength so quickly. In spite of his illness, Brad and Carrie feel they experienced a blessing they will never forget. Brad and Carrie believe it was more than the doctors and antibiotics that stopped the dreadful bacterial infection. The couple feels it was the intervention of God that alerted Carrie to take quick action. God's healing hand did the rest.

Brad has experienced several close calls in his life. Some were from illness, others from extreme danger. Through each one, he has known God's help and presence.

"Not only does He help me each day," says Brad, "I believe God gave me a guardian angel from the moment I was born."

JESUS, THY BOUNDLESS LOVE TO ME

O love, how cheering is Thy ray!
All pain before thy presence flies;
Care, anguish, sorrow, melt away
Wherever thy healing beams arise.
O Jesus, nothing may I see,
Nothing desire or seek, but Thee!
O, draw me, Saviour, after Thee;
So shall I run and never tire;
With gracious words still comfort me;
Be Thou my hope, my sole desire,
Free me from every weight; nor fear
Nor sin can come, if Thou art here.

PAUL GERHARDT, 1653,
TRANSLATED BY JOHN WESLEY, 1739

Thank You for Your goodness and blessings, Lord. Your mercy and kindness surpass all. During these trying times I turn to You. I am amazed how You used different people in my life to intervene and help me safely through. I praise You, Lord, for working so many things out and caring for me. Thank You for being with me from the very day I was born and for how You are with me all my life.

BECAUSE OF. . .

"For where two or three come together in my name, there am I with them."

MATTHEW 18:20 NIV

TWO MOTHERS, ONE PRAYER

The phone rattled a long, startling ring. Laverne bolted from a restless nap on the couch and stared at the still-cradled receiver. Would this be another prank call or a long-awaited answer?

Laverne and John's fifteen-year-old daughter

Chelsie had disappeared two months before. She had seemed happy, active in school, sports, and church. However, her parents sensed something was wrong. Chelsie wouldn't talk with them about her problems. What was happening?

Laverne cautiously answered the phone. Wrong number. Or was it? There was a long pause with no voice, then a click. Laverne shuddered and replaced the receiver. She threw herself on the couch and sobbed uncontrollably.

"Oh, Chelsie, Chelsie," she cried into the pillow. "I don't even know if you're alive."

Laverne and John tapped every resource they could think of to locate their beloved daughter: police, the news media, posters, letters. Most important, they asked friends and family to pray. Laverne especially coveted the prayers of her dear friend Jennifer.

Exhausted now, paperwork lying by her side, Laverne finally stretched out on the couch and rested. Her thoughts turned to the Lord as she began to pray. "Father," she sobbed through clenched teeth, "I've prayed constantly for help. I still haven't received an answer. Lord, *please* hear our prayers."

More tears spilled, but now Laverne felt the sweet presence of the Lord. She remembered her last conversation with Jennifer. Jennifer's son Adam had disappeared four years earlier, when he was eighteen. Jennifer didn't even know if Adam was still alive. Would it be the same with Chelsie?

God helped Laverne recall what Jennifer had said: "A prayer pact is formed between us for our kids, Laverne, so don't fear. God knows the needs of both of them. Let's trust and thank Him daily for answers and help to come."

God's presence grew stronger. Laverne began to pray again. This time she lifted her heart and hands in praise to God for the answers to Jennifer's and her prayers. An indescribable strength filled her entire being. She felt as though God carried her above the worries and problems, as though He was seeing her through her uncertainties and fear.

Two weeks passed. Each time Laverne felt anxious, she closed her eyes and imagined herself lifting her daughter up and giving her to God. She quoted promise after promise from her Bible of how God cares. She thanked and praised Him repeatedly for His love and compassion.

One evening the phone rang. A timid voice came over the line. "Mom? Mommy? I want to come home."

After a long talk with her cherished daughter, Laverne hung up the phone, overjoyed. The first thing she did was praise God for answered prayer. Then she called her husband, John, and her friend Jennifer.

Laverne and John's friends and family joined them in giving thanks for answered prayer. Jennifer was especially happy. One of their prayed-for children had returned home safely. Laverne and Jennifer kept trusting and praising God now more than ever for His help in finding Adam.

Adam had been a model child. But in his senior year, he began running with a drinking crowd. One thing led to another. Soon Adam slipped into alcoholism. Rather than bringing shame to his family, he left home, planning never to return.

After four years, Adam ended up on the streets of Los Angeles. Alcohol and drugs had consumed his life. His six-foot-three frame dwindled to skin draped over bones. Each day he became weaker, sleeping wherever he could. People stepped over and around him on the busy streets, obviously fearful of going too close or getting involved. Little by little Adam became almost too weak to breathe. He tried to move but could find no more strength.

Far away, Jennifer and Laverne prayed more intensely than ever and offered praise to God for His coming help. Powerful prayers skyrocketed across the country. Mark, a dedicated street minister, spotted Adam huddled and shaking in a downtown unused doorway. God spoke to Mark's heart and urged him to do something. Mark quickly reached down and gathered the foul-smelling, dying young man in his strong arms and carried him to a nearby mission.

Medical help rapidly kicked in. The ID Adam carried provided Jennifer's phone number. She was called immediately, informed of her son's location, and told he might be dying. Mother and son were reunited in a Los Angeles hospital.

Eventually, Adam successfully completed a drug/alcohol treatment program with much prayer backing him up. Chelsie renewed her commitment to God and is now happily married. Adam returned home. He is successfully employed and helps his mother with expenses and maintenance on their home.

Laverne and Jennifer look back and often thank God for answered prayers and continuing new victories.

O LORD, OUR LORD

Thy mighty works and wondrous grace
    Thy glory,
    Lord, proclaim.
O Lord, our Lord, in all the earth
    How excellent Thy name!

THE PSALTER, 1912

Thank You, again, dear Father for how You wondrously answered our urgent prayers. They were so personal, we couldn't bring them to a large group of believers. Although our numbers were small, we thank You for being with us.

Thank You for how You directed us and performed Your miraculous will to meet our needs. We praise You for Your wise and perfect plans and the way You surrounded us during this time with Your unwavering love and presence. When we became anxious and wanted to take back the burdens, You reminded us to leave them with You.

Thank You for Your comforting Holy Spirit, even when there were only two or three of us praying. Because of Your faithful love and care, we will praise Your name forever.

All the Days of My Life

LOOKING BACK

I waited patiently for the LORD; And He inclined to me, And heard my cry. He has put a new song in my mouth— Praise to our God; Many will see it and fear, And will trust in the LORD. PSALM 40:1, 3 NKJV

CHANGING TIDES

Small shells crunched into the pebbled sand beneath Rose's feet as she walked the Jamestown beach. Her legs felt weighted down after trudging only a few miles.

Rose sat on a log and gazed across the water. The sound looked as calm as a lake. The outgoing tide revealed a small spit where seagulls rested in partial sunlight. It was so quiet, Rose could hear boat motors from miles away and an occasional passing car from the street behind her.

The tide was out, making it possible for blue heron to elegantly stand in shallow water a safe distance from shore. How she would love to see them fly. Winds blowing the tide and ripples caused the sea life to continually adjust to nature's rhythm. Rose breathed deeply and filled her lungs with the clean, salty air.

A purple-shaded mountain range surrounded

most of the area as far as she could see. To her left, the long Dungeoness Spit stretched its huge finger out into the water for about twelve miles. She pulled out her binoculars to get a better look. Near the end of the spit, she could see a well-kept lighthouse. Its white paint and red trim shone brightly in the sun, in contrast to the surrounding blue sky and water.

Rose stirred the toe of her tennis shoe in the sand. The beachfront was changing as she sat there. She had been told when the storms come in, the strong waves could move ten-foot logs up and down the beach. Rose thought of the changes she, too, was constantly facing. Like the sea life, she had to continually develop a rhythm through wavering ups and downs and readjustments, while God's constant, gentle leading rippled through her everyday life—cleansing, shifting, and refreshing her.

Rose reached into her backpack and pulled out her journal, pen, and small Bible. They went almost everywhere with her like best friends. She began to read: *"To everything there is a season, a time for every purpose under heaven"* (Ecclesiastes 3:1 NKJV).

As Rose read some of her journal's log of events from her life, she could clearly see God's hand at work. She read about prayers being answered during the ups and downs through the past years. Monstrous problems had been solved. Huge splinters that felt as big as the seashore logs had been removed. Sometimes Rose had felt battered by troubles and wondered if she would survive. But now she could see how God's finger had created a long protecting bulwark for her, buffering her from harsh storms.

In her darkest hours when she thought she would crash against the rocks, the lighthouse of God's Word helped her find the way. When pressures fogged her thinking and she didn't know which way to turn, she remembered His speaking to her heart. Like a foghorn cutting through the murky air, God's unmistakable voice had cut through uncertainties.

Rose turned to a clean page in her journal and began writing: "I don't know what the future holds, Lord, but I know You are here every step of the way. Guarding. Guiding. Keeping."

AWAKE, MY SOUL,
TO JOYFUL LAYS

Awake, my soul, to joyful lays,
And sing thy great Redeemer's praise;
He justly claims a song from me—
His lovingkindness, O how free!
Lovingkindness, lovingkindness,
His lovingkindness, O how free!

When trouble, like a gloomy cloud,
Has gathered thick and thundered loud,
He near my soul has always stood—
His lovingkindness, O how good!
Lovingkindness, lovingkindness,
His lovingkindness, O how good!

SAMUEL MEDLEY, 1782

I WILL REMEMBER
YOUR FAITHFULNESS

Through my life's changing sands of time, I look back and recall Your countless blessings, Father. Thank You for being with me through all my years.

I praise You for Your faithfulness in helping me to adjust to life's changes and for granting me strength to trust in You. Your love has always been there for me. Even when I felt abandoned and believed things were hopeless, You helped me through. Afterward, I looked back and often saw how You had worked.

Thank You for Your unchanging love. It goes above the mountains and beyond the skies to help me. It reaches into the deepest sea, where You stretch out Your hand and lift me up.

Because I see what You have done for me in the past, I look to the future without fear. Thank You, Lord God. In all my days I will always remember Your faithfulness.

PRESSING FORWARD

"But whoever lives by the truth comes into the light, so that it may be seen plainly that what he has done has been done through God."

JOHN 3:21 NIV

Hot, sticky air smothered the Kansas farm. Late afternoon was fast approaching. Due to the heat, Riley, his wife, Amy, and their children would water the animals and fowl one more time before dinner, and then they would have ice-cold lemonade under the trees.

Everyone finished except six-year-old Michael, who still had to water the horses. He must have been playing with his pocket-sized flashlight instead.

Before Riley could check on his son, the hot air grew deadly silent. Not even a bird was to be heard. A black funnel showed in the distance—a tornado was coming. The family knew what to do.

Amy and the children ran for the storm cellar. Riley sprinted toward the barn, frantically calling Michael's name, but the father was too late.

Wind, dirt, and debris flew around Riley with driving force. Like second nature, the father dove for an irrigation ditch near him and lay flat.

"Please, Lord, protect Michael and my family," Riley shouted.

The storm passed as quickly as it came. All was deathly still. Amy and the children ran toward Riley. The house remained standing, but the barn lay in shambles. Where was their dear Michael?

Everyone ran to the demolished barn, calling Michael's name. No answer. All they could see in the rubble was darkness. Was there any glimmer of hope for Michael to be alive and unharmed? They shot up another quick prayer for help.

"Look!" Amy shouted. She pointed to one corner of the barn still standing.

Riley bent down and peered between the boards, shielding his eyes from the sun. On, off, on, off flashed a little light.

"It's Michael!" cheered Riley. "He's alive."

For what seemed like forever, the family carefully moved one board after another. They could hear coughing and sputtering. Everyone cried for joy.

At last Riley exposed the barn's corner. Down in the feed bin huddled Michael. The blowing dust had choked the little boy's voice, but when Riley gently lifted his son, Michael snuggled close in his father's arms, safe and sound.

The family made their way across the barnyard to their house. Never mind the barn. Thank God they were all safe.

Michael smiled at his dad and mother. "It's okay, Mom and Pop," he whispered, "I trusted God to take care of me." He pulled out his flashlight from his pocket. "I turned on my light and just let it shine and shine and shine."

God wants us to press on and continue being a blessing for Him. Whenever things become difficult, He reminds us He is our Light, shining in the darkness. He is our hope for the future. All we need do is trust Him and let our lights shine and shine. He will take care of us.

JESUS BIDS US SHINE

Jesus bids us shine, with a clear, pure light,
Like a little candle burning in the night;
In this world of darkness we must shine,
You in your small corner, and I in mine.

SUSAN WARNER, 1819–1885

YOU ARE MY GLIMMER OF HOPE

When everything seems hopeless, You are my glimmer of hope, Lord. I will trust in You with all my heart. You are my light and my salvation. I know I won't remain in darkness, when I follow You. Thank You for how Your light and mine will shine, wherever we go.

And I
Will Dwell
in the House
of the Lord

GOD'S CHURCH

LORD, I have loved the habitation of Your
house, And the place where Your glory dwells.

PSALM 26:8 NKJV

JULIANNA'S LOVESEEDS

Sixteen-year-old Julianna wasn't very excited about taking a trip with her parents from Pennsylvania to Washington's west coast. Hours of riding in the car with her parents and not knowing anyone sounded boring. Her family had planned the cross-country trip for a year, though, and she knew she must make the best of it.

Shortly before leaving, Julianna heard a knock on her bedroom door. Her mother entered and sat by Julianna on the edge of her bed.

"I have something that will change this whole trip for you, Julianna." Her mother handed her a package of flower seeds. "Think of ways to spread these wherever we go. Let's call them loveseeds. Each time you spread them, pray for the people they touch."

Julianna and her parents climbed into the car and prayed for safety before pulling out of the driveway. Julianna loved the Lord, but she was having a difficult time finding her way through her changing life. Along with everything else, she simply couldn't see the meaning of going to church. What was church, anyway? But everywhere they went, Julianna dropped a pinch of seeds: vacant lots, along the freeways, in the desert. Somehow, she was beginning to enjoy the project, and she wondered if the seeds would ever grow. She found herself asking God for a little rain to help them along. When she ran out of seeds, she used her spending money to buy more. She purchased wildflowers, sunflowers, daisies, plus whatever she thought would work.

One time while they were in a restaurant Julianna noticed a little boy crying. Without thinking, she got up, went over to the table, and asked the parents if she could give him a package of seeds. The boy was thrilled, anxious for his parents to take him home and help him plant them. Julianna remembered what her mother had said, and she prayed for him as she and her parents traveled on.

Each Sunday Julianna's family stopped somewhere for church. She was surprised at the kinship she felt with Christian teenagers, wherever they happened to be. Each time she made a new friend, Julianna left a package of seeds and her address so they could keep in touch and pray for one another.

By the time they reached the West Coast, she had begun to realize what the church was really all about. Her parents had often told her some day she would see the true church—not just a building, but Christians, who were part of God's family.

When Julianna and her family returned home,

she was surprised. Several letters for her had come from all across the United States. She would keep in touch with her new friends and hopefully see them again.

Ten years later, Julianna and her husband started out on the same drive from the West Coast. The two of them had met in church during her well-remembered family trip. The seeds she left him, frequent letters over the years, along with attending a college together on the West Coast, caused their friendship to blossom into love and marriage. Now they were driving to New York to visit her parents.

A big smile crossed her face as Julianna and her husband noticed a variety of volunteer flowers growing here and there along their trip. More than anything, she was thankful for how God had taught her to spread spiritual loveseeds. Because of those seeds, she now understood what God's church really was.

BRINGING IN THE SHEAVES

Sowing in the morning, sowing seeds
   of kindness,
Sowing in the noontide and the dewy eve;
Waiting for the harvest, and the time of reaping,
We shall come rejoicing, bringing in the sheaves.

Sowing in the sunshine, sowing in the shadows,
Fearing neither clouds nor winter's
   chilling breeze;
By and by the harvest, and the labor ended,
We shall come rejoicing, bringing in the sheaves.

KNOWLES SHAW, 1874

THANK YOU FOR YOUR CHURCH

When I go up the steps of my church, Father, I feel a warmth in my heart. I'm ready to worship You. Your presence in the service blesses me and prepares me to face another week, so I can go about my duties.

Thank You, too, for the extended part of Your church, Father, as I get to know Christians wherever I go. It's exciting. It's like meeting a long-lost cousin. When we are Your children, we truly are part of Your holy family.

Thank You for adopting me into Your family and making me a part of the kingdom of God.

PRAYER CLOSET

"But you, when you pray, go into your room, and when you have shut your door, pray to your Father who is in the secret place; and your Father who sees in secret will reward you openly."

MATTHEW 6:6 NKJV

HANDS ON THE WORKBENCH

Tim's garage workbench served a lot of purposes. It sometimes held parts of a broken toy while Tim's son or daughter waited patiently for experienced fingers to make it like new. There were days when it held all kinds of tools, while Tim worked on the house or car. Tender shoots of flowers, berries, and vegetables were given their starts in tiny pots on Tim's workbench, later to grow and flourish in the yard.

Tim enjoyed the times in his garage. But the best times of all were when the garage became his prayer closet, and the workbench became his altar. There, with his hands folded on his bench, Tim took broken hearts to God and waited patiently while God fixed them. Tim brought newborn Christians to the Lord and prayed for them to grow. Sometimes the needs for which he prayed were personal, for Tim alone.

The workbench became Tim's favorite spot to pray. The worn wood seemed to yield as his hands pressed there each day. Time stood still whenever the simple garage and workbench became a prayer closet with God.

SWEET HOUR OF PRAYER

Sweet hour of prayer! sweet hour of prayer!
The joys I feel, the bliss I share,
Of those whose anxious spirits burn
With strong desires for thy return!
With such I hasten to the place
Where God my Savior shows His face,
And gladly take my station there,
And wait for thee, sweet hour of prayer!

W. W. WALFORD, 1845

MY QUIET PLACE

Father, I find my quiet place waiting for me as I take my early morning walk. My children still sleep soundly with my husband near. Thank You for this quiet time with You.

I pause along this walking trail and sit on a bench. Your blessed quiet surrounds me as the rising sun and birds join as one.

I love You, Lord Jesus. You show me so much good as I pray. Your face shines upon me and You fill my heart with joy as You and I have time to talk—and listen. I thank You for Your blessings; I bring my needs to You. I learn from You so I can be the person You want me to be.

I must go now about my duties. Remain with me, I pray, through this day. Tonight we may be able to have more time together when the sun goes down and all is quiet again.

WAY OF LIFE

*But the mercy of the L*ORD *is from everlasting to everlasting On those who fear Him, And His righteousness to children's children, To such as keep His covenant, And to those who remember His commandments to do them.*

PSALM 103:17–18 NKJV

WELL-WORN PATH

The path Jesus leads us on isn't meant to be taken only once.

We reach the glorious decision to follow Him and our spirits soar. We digest the Bible's teachings like tasty life-giving morsels of bread. We experience His blessings and drink of His cleansing fountain. But a piece of bread, a drink of water, and rest for the body only strengthen us for one day. In the same way, Jesus wants us to fortify our souls and minds when we come to Him in prayer again and again. Only then do we remain strong Christians.

God wants us to read our Bibles and pray often. Each time we do, the Savior provides us with spiritual energy that recharges us to go on. After we rise from our knees, we are able to follow the hem of His robe again.

Every day is a brand new adventure with God. Each one begins with His starting us on the holy path once more, aligned with His will. Spending time in prayer becomes a way of life.

It's never too soon or too late to begin following the path God has for you. Choose it soon. Feel His strength and glory. Enjoy reading His words in your Bible. See what a wonderful life He has in the making for you.

After you have tried this path with Jesus for awhile and made it a way of life, you will look back on your well-worn trail and see how it has become the best road you could have ever taken: a life that's free, filled with joy and victory.

TAKE TIME TO BE HOLY

Take time to be holy, speak oft with thy Lord;
Abide in Him always, and feed on His Word.
Make friends of God's children, help those who
    are weak,
Forgetting in nothing His blessing to seek.

WILLIAM DUNN LONGSTAFF, CIRCA 1882

You are so dear to me, Lord, while we walk this path of life together. How priceless You are to me. You are my way of life. How grateful I am for Your unfailing love. Each day, I find refuge in the safekeeping of Your protecting wings.

Whenever I come to You, I feast on Your Word and drink from Your rivers of cleansing delight. I praise You, Lord, for You are my living Fountain, giving me abundant life.

Forever

MOVING ON WITH GOD

Be strong and take heart, all you who hope in the LORD.　　　　　　　PSALM 31:24 NIV

Be joyful in hope, patient in affliction, faithful in prayer.　　　　　　ROMANS 12:12 NIV

RAINBOW OF HOPE

Seattle, Washington, has a reputation for its rain. We who live here grow webbed feet, so to speak. Kids play in the rain, while we adults always keep our umbrellas handy. Rain doesn't slow us down much; we just slop around in it as we scurry here and there.

When we have a few days without a sprinkle, we find ourselves wrinkling our noses at the smelly air. We look up into the nearly cloudless sky, stretch out our palms, shrug our shoulders, and say, "Well, where's that nice cleansing rain?"

I don't like the slow, drizzly kind of rain that goes on for days, but I love the shower bursts in the afternoons. The rain pours like crazy, while the sun lazily slips toward the western horizon. I find myself running to the window, out in the yard, or even into the street to spot a new, glorious rainbow in the eastern sky. I grab the camera. One more rainbow to enter my photo albums.

We all face discouraging times when the long drizzle of uncertainties shadows over us. We wonder when we will see past the clouds.

Then right in the midst of it all, the Son of God breaks through our gloom and apprehension and plants a Scripture with delightful promises of His love. One of my friends calls God's promises rainbows of love, just for us.

Like rainbows, we can't touch His promises. Sometimes we aren't able to visualize where life is going. As the rains cloud our vision, God filters through it all and reminds us He is still there, loving and helping. He gives us a pact, His covenant. He has sealed it with the crimson blood of His Son, Jesus Christ, assuring us He never leaves nor forsakes us.

The next time uncertain rains fall, remember to cling to the hope God gives and look for His rainbow of promises. Don't be afraid to move forward with God and follow His leading; after all, He is the One Who made it all. His sure and capable hands will provide you a future of love, comfort, hope, joy, and eternal life.

GOD MOVES IN A MYSTERIOUS WAY

God moves in a mysterious way
His wonders to perform;
He plants His footsteps in the sea
And rides upon the storm.

Ye fearful saints, fresh courage take;
The clouds ye so much dread
Are big with mercy and shall break
In blessings on your head.

WILLIAM COWPER, 1774

MOVING FORWARD WITH YOU

In You I put my trust and hope, Lord God, for You are the One Who holds my future. Thank You for the plans You have for me. I may shake in my boots, but I will still move forward and obey Your will. I behold Your presence as You gaze upon my transparent soul. You know me well and can see far better than I the best ways for me to go.

I look up with steadfast trust and thank You for how Your mercy and love surround me. I praise You for helping me to move forward with You.

FOREVER WILLING

"And if anyone gives even a cup of cold water to one of these little ones because he is my disciple, I tell you the truth, he will certainly not lose his reward." MATTHEW 10:42 NIV

A Willing Spirit

She suffers from poor health, but never gives up. Sometimes walking becomes too painful, and she's forced to use a wheelchair or walker. When she's able to come to church, though, she's there. She's always willing to listen to the concerns of others, to care and pray for them. She doesn't sing in a choir, teach a class, or give dynamic speeches. She's just approachable, loving, compassionate.

Even when she's home, she's helping others. She sends notes to the sick, the bereaved, and the lonely. She sews banners for the Sunday school department. She helps with paperwork. She shows a huge amount of love and cooks great dishes for church potlucks.

Thank you, Sharon, for being a willing spirit for the Lord!

How fortunate we all are to have the loving, willing spirits who bless us each day.

Forth in Thy Name, O Lord

Forth in Thy name, O Lord, I go,
My daily labor to pursue;
Thee, only Thee, resolved to know
In all I think or speak or do.

CHARLES WESLEY, 1749

MAKE ME FOREVER WILLING

When You call me, Father, make me eager to do Your will. Help me to be dependable and finish the work You set before me. Let me jump in with eager enthusiasm to complete the task, as though I'm doing it for You.

If my spirit grows weary and my body becomes tired, grant me the strength I need. Help me to be willing to listen, love, and care.

I'm ready to do anything for You, Father. Please stay close so we can be a blessing together.

NEW CHALLENGES

This is love for God: to obey his commands. And his commands are not burdensome, for everyone born of God overcomes the world. This is the victory that has overcome the world, even our faith. Who is it that overcomes the world? Only he who believes that Jesus is the Son of God.

1 JOHN 5:3–5 NIV

He was born to a poor Revolutionary War veteran turned farmer. He never heard prayer or the Bible read in his parents' home. He figured out how to pray on his own as a child and never owned a Bible until he was grown.

He learned to hunt at an early age and became an expert shot. He was strong and quick; the boy could outrun, outjump, and outthrow all of his friends. As he grew older, he became accomplished at swimming and sailing. He excelled in his learning in a one-room schoolhouse and completed his basic education at sixteen years of age.

The teenager furthered his studies at Hamilton Oneida Institute, now known as Hamilton College. While there, Principal Seth Norton awakened the youth's love for music. Principal Norton taught him to sing and to play the violin and cello.

Still in his teenage years, he started teaching. He used his first earnings to purchase himself a cello. His students loved and respected him for his enthusiasm for music and the way he participated with them in sports. His parents, however, showed little interest in his accomplishments.

Later, he considered enlisting in the navy. He heard more profanity during that time than he had heard in his entire life. To make matters worse, he was approached by a young, pretty street woman. When he realized her intent, his cheeks burned. Before he could catch himself, he burst into tears for the woman. His sorrow moved her to shame and she also wept. He chose not to join the navy.

After several years of college and teaching, he bought a Bible. The more he read, the more he wanted to know God on a personal level.

At age twenty-nine, he accepted Christ as his Savior. Need for intellectual proof of God left, like shucked old clothing, tossed, never taken back.

He often remembered the incident years before with the street woman. He regretted he wasn't a Christian then; if he had been, he could have shared the gospel with her.

Not long after, he felt God's call to the ministry. He fervently preached a salvation message, blunt, honest, with no holds barred.

Revival broke out wherever he spoke. When people listened to him speak, they had to either accept or reject Christ. The Holy Spirit worked with such strength that even when the young preacher never said a word, folks gave their hearts to God.

Charles Grandison Finney accepted God's challenge and won countless souls to Him throughout the nation. He inspired many to enter the ministry during turbulent times. Most of all, he left us a record that tells of the transforming power of God.

This same power is still available to us now during our troubled times, more than one hundred years later.

The Master's Call

Behold, the Master now is calling
For reapers brave and true;
The golden harvest fields are waiting,
But labourers are few.

Go, bid the poor with joy and gladness
The feast of love to share;
And He the Bread of Life Eternal
Will make them welcome there.

Go forth, with patience, love and kindness;
And in the Master's name,
The blessed news of free salvation
To all the world proclaim!

JULIA STERLIND, LATE 1800s

I Accept Your Challenge

No matter the challenge You place before me, Lord,
I'll follow. If You call me to the highest mountain, I'll
go. If You lead me across the seas, I will obey.

When the task becomes difficult, I pray You will
go before me and give me courage not to quit. Though
I may not always feel brave, Lord, I know You are
strong where I am weak. For this reason, I will trust
You with all my heart and follow.

I'm ready to accept Your challenge, Lord. With enthusiasm and vision for the future, I'll go forth and follow You.

NEW ETERNAL HOME

"I am the way and the truth and the life. No one comes to the Father except through me."

JOHN 14:6 NIV

"Do not let your hearts be troubled. Trust in God; trust also in me. In my Father's house are many rooms; if it were not so, I would have told you. I am going there to prepare a place for you. And if I go and prepare a place for you, I will come back and take you to be with me that you may also be where I am."

JOHN 14:1–3 NIV

WELCOME HOME

Whenever I think of heaven, a deep, homesick feeling stirs within me. I feel I have been there before my time on this earth began. There is an overpowering love drawing me to run and fall into my heavenly Father's arms.

Like Martha, I want to sit at the feet of my Lord and ask all the questions I've accumulated during my stay on earth. One by one, I believe He'll help me understand the answers.

Perhaps many Christians feel this way who know the Father well. We communicate with Him daily and sense His loving presence. Although I love my husband, family, and friends here, there is a deeper, fuller love I feel for my Father in heaven.

What will heaven be like? The Bible says there will be no more sin or violence, sickness or pain, no tears or grief. We often grow weary of fending off these things that cause anguish and stress. We long for a carefree, eternal life with God in heaven. What a delight it will be when we get to see our Christian loved ones and friends who have gone home before us!

But there is more to heaven than this. The glorious, awesome Triune of God the Father, God the Son, and God the Holy Spirit is there. Heaven will be more than a blessed revival or camp meeting. We will actually get to meet Him face-to-face!

As I fall before Him in reverence, I can imagine Jesus, my Savior, stepping forward, bending down, and taking my hand. As He helps me to my feet, I may hear Him say, "It's all right, My child. I paid the price for your sins. Welcome home."

The Home of the Soul

I will sing you a song of the beautiful land,
The faraway home of the soul,
Where no storms ever beat on the glittering
    strand,
While the years of eternity roll.

Oh, that home of the soul! In my visions and
    dreams
Its bright jasper walls I can see,
Till I fancy but thinly the veil intervenes
Between the fair city and me.

That unchangeable home is for you and for me,
Where Jesus of Nazareth stands;
The King of all kingdoms for ever is He,
And He holdeth our crowns in His hands.

Mrs. E. H. Gates, late 1800s

Someday I Will Dwell with You

Father, although I love my life here with my family
and friends, I long to be with You. Your Bible tells
me when I'm in heaven with You, there will be no
more anger, sin, sadness, sickness, or death; neither
will there be fear, grieving, or pain.

In one way I cling to my dear ones, my physical life, and things familiar. In another, I feel displaced, as though I'm only put here for a little while. I look forward to when I can come home to Your holy city. There I can worship You in Your tabernacle where You dwell. There, You will wipe away every tear and take away my pain. There, I can run to Your arms and tell You how much I love You. There, I will be home with You at last.

I hope You will be able to say, *"Well done, good and faithful servant"* (Matthew 25:23 NKJV).

A GAELIC BLESSING

May there always be work for your hands to do.
May your purse always hold a coin or two.
May the sun always shine warm on your
    window pane.
May a rainbow be certain to follow each rain,
May the hand of a friend always be near you.
And may God fill your heart with blessings
    to cheer you.

OTHER BOOKS BY
ANITA CORRINE DONIHUE

If you enjoyed *When God Sees Me Through,* be sure to look for these other books by Anita Corrine Donihue at your local Christian bookstore:

When I'm on My Knees
The highly popular collection of devotional thoughts on prayer, especially for women.
    ISBN 1-55748-976-9. . . . . \$4.97

When I'm Praising God
Anita's second book in the series, celebrating the spiritual joy of praise.
    ISBN 1-57748-447-9. . . . . \$4.97

When I'm in His Presence
Anita's third book, encouraging women to look for God's working in their everyday lives.
    ISBN 1-57748-665-X \$4.97

ALSO AVAILABLE:
When I'm on My Knees Prayer Journal
Favorite selections from *When I'm on My Knees,* plus ample journaling space for your prayer requests and praise notes.
    ISBN 1-57748-836-9. . . . . \$4.97

Available wherever books are sold.
Or order from:

Barbour Publishing, Inc.
P.O. Box 719
Uhrichsville, OH 44683
http://www.barbourbooks.com

If you order by mail, add \$2.00 to your order for shipping.
Prices are subject to change without notice.